ANDRE BRETON

by

MARY ANN CAWS

An individual treatment of Breton's major works, with emphasis on the themes of language as a revolutionary and "alchemical" work, on the complex oppositions of love, political commitment, and personal solitude, on poetry as the place where the contraries are reconciled and the place of inner spectacle, not for the reader but for the poet alone. The discussion of the motifs of Surrealism such as disorientation and desire, indications and analogy, openness, doubt, and risk, refusal, freedom and necessity, intuition and the marvelous image, is never detached from the particular setting where they occur, in keeping with Breton's stress on the *situation*.

Equal attention is given to certain recurring phrases in particular and to the style of Surrealism in general—as it is deliberately extreme, repetitive, alternating, and ambiguous, in keeping with the Surrealist theory it develops. Finally, style and theory are linked with personality, and Breton himself is seen as the voluntary fanatic, both self-willed and heroic.

TWAYNE'S WORLD AUTHORS SERIES

A Survey of the World's Literature

Sylvia E. Bowman, Indiana University

GENERAL EDITOR

FRANCE

Maxwell A. Smith, Guerry Professor of French, Emeritus
The University of Chattanooga
Former Visiting Professor in Modern Languages
The Florida State University

EDITOR

André Breton

(TWAS 117)

TWAYNE'S WORLD AUTHORS SERIES (TWAS)

The purpose of TWAS is to survey the major writers
—novelists, dramatists, historians, poets, philosophers,
and critics—of the nations of the world. Among the
national literatures covered are those of Australia,
Canada, China, Eastern Europe, France, Germany,
Greece, Italy, Japan, Latin America, New Zealand,
Poland, Russia, Scandinavia, Spain, and the African
nations, as well as Hebrew, Yiddish, and Latin Classi-
cal literature. This survey is complemented by
Twayne's United States Authors Series and
English Authors Series.

The intent of each volume in these series is to present
a critical-analytical study of the works of the writer;
to include biographical and historical material that
may be necessary for understanding, appreciation,
and critical appraisal of the writer; and to present all
material in clear, concise English—but not to vitiate
the scholarly content of the work by doing so.

André Breton

By MARY ANN CAWS

Hunter College
of the City University of New York

Twayne Publishers, Inc.   ::   New York

ANDRE BRETON

To Peter

Liberté couleur d'homme (Liberty color of man)

"Il n'y a pas à sortir de là"

L'amour, la poésie, l'art, c'est par leur seul ressort que la confiance reviendra, que la pensée humaine parviendra à reprendre le large. (Love, poetry, art, it is only by their help that confidence will reappear, that human thought will succeed in starting out once more.)

Arcane 17

ABOUT THE AUTHOR

B.A., Bryn Mawr, M.A., Yale, Ph.D. University of Kansas.

Taught at the University of Kansas, Barnard College, and Sarah Lawrence: now Assistant Professor of French at Hunter College of the City University of New York and a member of the doctoral faculty of the Graduate Center.

Articles, reviews, and *explications de texte*, mostly in the field of Dada and Surrealism, in *French Review, Yale French Studies, L'Esprit créateur, The Explicator, Contemporary Literature, Modern Language Quarterly, Romance Notes, Novel, Books Abroad, Romanic Review* and the *Cahiers Dada Surréalisme*.

Author of *Surrealism and the Literary Imagination: a study of Breton and Bachelard*, The Hague, Mouton, 1966, and *The Poetry of Dada and Surrealism: Aragon, Breton, Tzara, Eluard, Desnos*, Princeton, Princeton University Press, 1970.

Preface

J'ai plus confiance dans ce moment actuel de ma pensée que dans tout ce qu'on tentera de faire signifier à une oeuvre achevée, à une vie humaine parvenue à son terme. (I have more confidence in this present moment of my thought than in all the meaning people will try to give to a complete work, to a human life once it is finished—*Manifestes,* p. 95).

"This present moment of my thought": no book on Breton can pretend (in either sense of the word) to make a résumé of his thought, his life, or his work without insulting him in the gravest manner possible. He wanted all these to seem, even from a distance, as transparent as a crystal of rock salt, but he also demanded that his works be left *open.* To put an explanation on any of his writing is to set it within limits, to close it off, and such a thing would do injustice to the ideal metaphors of swinging doors, communicating vessels, and connecting wires which haunt all the texts, theories, and attitudes of the Surrealist movement he led.

Surrealism insists on the *latent content* and not on the manifest content, on the *interior necessity* and not on the exterior influences, on the *interior model* and not on the exterior representation. To look at this "mental situation" from the outside is already an enterprise suspect to the adherents of the movement, and to a certain extent, justifiably so. But to concentrate, for instance, on the "influences" upon it or on its own reverberations in "influencing" fields beyond it, is even less acceptable to its essential spirit. Surrealism insists that every act is its own justification, is unique and *dissimilar.*

In his "Lettre aux voyantes" of 1929, Breton urged the recognition of an *absolute possibility,* which was to furnish the basis of a moral truth. An epoch lived through may be more or less terrible, but to emphasize unduly the exterior variations detracts,

like an undue emphasis on the past, from the all-important openness to the future. A device which claims to predict the so-
called variability of the weather or of the times[1] is in error,
for neither the past moments nor the present unrest (or calm) can
determine the time to come: it is rather the latter which makes itself felt as a guiding force in the present:

already the man I will be takes the man I am by the throat, but the
man I have been leaves me in peace (*Manifestes*, p. 232).

The essential of man, Breton stated again and again, is that he can
go beyond his condition. The freedom from all limits which is
Surrealism's goal would not be best served by concentrating on the
circumstances of Surrealism or on its history.[2]

After a very brief discussion, therefore, of the *position* of Breton
and Surrealism and an even briefer one of the variations of that
position, the order of this book will relate only to the texts left by
Breton. In his *Nadja* he made a point of setting down facts and
details "without a preestablished order." Since that is impossible
here within the limits necessarily set, the discussion will proceed
by the limits Breton himself accepted, not the chronological
limits[3] but the simple limits of form: manifestoes, essays, longer
essays in book form (where *Nadja* is included as a novelistic
essay), and finally, poetry. A few indications about the reading
of Surrealist poetry precede the discussion of the themes and
style of Breton's poems. Within these poems themselves, the
themes already stated in preceding sections will reappear; poetry
is the privileged place of Surrealist encounter, at once the least
limited, and the most difficult.

In the two final sections, three short essays of great importance
will form the basis of a few concluding remarks on Breton's attitude toward the image and the imagination, the alchemical operation on language and the world, and the future of poetry.

Contents

Preface

Chronology

1. Life, Youth, Revolution   13

2. André Breton and Surrealism   17

3. Word and Image: *"à la lumière de l'image"*   22

4. *Les Pas perdus*   30

5. *Point du jour*   41

6. *La Clé des Champs*   48

7. *Le Surréalisme et la peinture*   57

8. Love, Madness, and Solitude   62

9. Poetry: *"lieu de reconciliation"*   87

10. Liberty: *"le coup d'aile"*   112

11. Conclusion   118

    Notes and References   121

    Bibliography   127

    Index   131

    Appendix: Reading a Surrealist Poem   134

Chronology

1896 Born in Tinchebray (Orne).

1915 After studies in medicine, Breton is mobilized. Serves in neuropsychiatric centers.

1919 *Mont de Piété.* With Louis Aragon and Philippe Soupault, founds *Littérature,* where the "first" Surrealist text appears, *Les Champs magnétiques* (Breton and Soupault).

1919-1921 Participates in the Mouvement Dada.

1921 Marries Simone Kahn.

1922 Takes over direction of *Littérature.* Hypnotic sleep experiments. Editor of *La Révolution surréaliste* (See his explanation: "Why I am assuming the editorship of *La Révolution surréaliste*").

1924 *Manifeste du surréalisme.* Opening of the Bureau de Recherches Surréalistes, rue de Grenelle. *Au Grand Jour,* pamphlet signed by the Surrealists.

1928 Publication of *Nadja.*

1929 Editor of *Le Surréalisme au service de la révolution;* period of association with the Communist party.

1930 *Deuxième Manifeste du surréalisme;* denunciation of Antonin Artaud and Robert Desnos. *L'Immaculée Conception* (with Paul Eluard), simulation of the language of certain nervous disorders.

1932 *Les Vases communicants, Le Revolver à cheveux blancs.* Pamphlet, *Misère de la poésie* (on the Aragon affair). Founding of the new magazine *Minotaure.*

1934 May 29, "La Nuit du tournesol": meets his second wife Jacqueline Lamba, under circumstances he had predicted 11 years earlier in the poem "Tournesol" (see *L'Amour fou*). *L'Air de l'eau.*

1935 Goes to the Canary Islands, and to Prague. Rupture with the Communist party.

1936 Organizes International Surrealist Exhibition in London.

1937 *L'Amour fou.*

1938 Organizes International Exhibition of Surrealism in Paris. Goes to Mexico, where he founds, with Leon Trotsky, the Fédération Internationale de l'Art Indépendant Révolutionnaire; Trotsky asks that Diego Rivera's name be substituted for his own on the manifesto.

1940 *Anthologie de l'humour noir.* Goes to Marseilles, writes *Fata Morgana* there.

1941 Leaves for New York. Speaker for Voice of America; founds *VVV* with Marcel Duchamp, David Hare, Max Ernst.

1942 International Exhibition of Surrealism in New York.

1945 *Arcane 17* (set in the Gaspé Peninsula). Marries Elisa Bindhoff. Visits Southwest (background for the *Ode à Charles Fourier*) and Haiti, where his lecture touches off a general strike.

1946 Returns to Paris.

1947 International Exhibition of Surrealism in Paris, Galerie Maeght. Manifestation at the lecture of Tristan Tzara, "Le Surréalisme et l'après-guerre," which accuses the Surrealists and mainly Breton of nonrelevance to political events. Publication of *Ode à Charles Fourier.*

1948 Adheres to Front Humain (which later become Citoyens du Monde).

1949 Exposes fake Rimbaud, "La Chasse spirituelle," on grounds of interior evidence (see essay "Flagrant Délit").[1]

1950 Refuses Grand Prix de la Ville de Paris.

1952 Founding of *Médium.*

1953 *La Clé des champs.*

1955 *Prolégomènes à un troisième manifeste ou non.* "Du Surréalisme en ses oeuvres vives."

1956 Founding of *Le Surréalisme, même.*

1960 Execution of the Last Will and Testament of the Marquis de Sade.

1961 Founding of *La Brêche, action surréaliste.*

1966 Breton dies in Paris.

(NOTE: Breton's contributions to, and collaboration with, several journals besides those mentioned is of prime importance— from *Nord-Sud* on. See the longer works on him for details.)

CHAPTER 1

Life, Youth, Revolution

I *Breton in the Present Tense*

Breton tells us very little of his childhood; it is not a matter of importance for him, or for us. Those accustomed to standard biographies and autobiographies, with an unfailing number of early scenes, tedious descriptions of parents, painful portraits of the child in family groups and school groups, may see this as an odd gap. But to the reader who is in the slightest acquainted with the Surrealist disposition, such standard equipment would seem at best satirical, and more probably, ludicrous. Few Surrealists lament knowing little of the life of Lautréamont: the silence serves his reputation and nourishes his legend. Thus, the cover illustration of Patrick Waldberg's book on Surrealism, representing the author as a small boy, is a superb example of para-Surrealist humor. And Breton was often accused of having no sense of humor (see his admission, quoted in Chapter 2, that he was "as tedious as the rain"). At all events, what counts in any study of Breton is not his physical whereabouts—whether he is living in the Hôtel des Grands Hommes or 42, rue Fontaine, whether he is in Canada or in Arizona—or even his encounters and adventures as such. Only his state of mind is significant; it is generally accepted that even when it is the most clearly turned out toward or against the world, Surrealism is essentially a way of perceiving and reacting, and that its interest lies as much in its own reactions and perceptions as in the situation which provokes them, if not more.

Of the period 1916–20, that is, the period immediately preceding the first surge of Surrealism, we are told more. Breton emerges during those four years from the influences of Mallarmé and Valéry, perhaps through the contact in the neuropsychiatric ward at Nantes with Jacques Vaché (see footnote 4, Chapter 3), who accuses the *"pohète"* [1] in him and succeeds in turning him away from the path of "estheticism" and "literature" toward a more revolutionary path. This evolution can be traced through the journals *Nord-Sud* and *Littérature* (whose title, as it is usually interpreted, is already satiric) toward *La Révolution surréaliste*. Breton's contact with Tristan Tzara and the Dada movement (1917–22) was certainly a decisive factor in his later development —whether or not it is considered *the* decisive factor depends on one's point of view. It is an indisputable fact that many of the themes and attitudes of Dada statements are found also in Surrealism, as will be apparent in this study. We may consider the encounter with Tzara and Dada itself to be, for the young men who were potential Surrealists, principally a state of readiness for the later development, as Breton would have us consider it; or we may take the view, as do some of the Dada sympathizers, that Breton builds up the legend of Vaché in order to reduce his apparent debt to Tzara and to Dada. Luckily, there is no way of settling such disputes. Like the deliberate omission of details about the youth of Breton, the uncertainty here contributes to the aura of Surrealism itself.

In any case, Breton participates until 1921 in the various Dada demonstrations and manifestations, usually called "negative," and then tries to hold a Congress for the Determination of the Modern Spirit, usually thought of as an attempt to give a "positive" or constructive basis to an endeavor which until that time had been more or less formless. The more "orthodox" Dadaists oppose such an idea as essentially non-Dada, and the friction which has been latent among certain members of differing tendencies comes to the surface. (To follow the various quarrels and changes of membership in this period and in successive periods is obviously beyond the scope of this study.)

For the next few years, the future Surrealist group, led by Breton, concentrates above all on techniques of communication with the unconscious (discussed in Chapter 4); this is the period of automatic writing, hypnotic sleeps, recitals of dreams, and the Bureau de Recherches Surréalistes. After the influence of Freud, the influence of Marx: the subsequent period, roughly from 1929 to 1935, when the Surrealists align themselves with the French Communist party, can be considered a more "practical" period (which is briefly discussed in Chapter 2).

During the war years, Breton, whose anthology of black humor is banned in Vichy France, goes first to Marseilles, then to New York to broadcast for the Voice of America. In New

York the Surrealist group with new members continues its meetings with enthusiasm, and Breton founds the journal *VVV* with David Hare. He travels widely (to the Southwest, to the Canary Islands, to Canada) and writes works of a more mystic inclination, in the vein of his *Fata Morgana* written before his departure from Marseilles. His *Ode à Charles Fourier* extols the *"sens de la fête"* (sense of the feast), with all its gnostic and communal implications as well as its more obvious ones (joy, passion), and his *Arcane 17,* written in the Gaspé Peninsula, is itself an ode to love and to the mysteries of the alchemical and the arcane.

On his return to France, Breton once more forms a Surrealist group, but is now under attack by Tzara and others for having chosen exile above resistance. Although the friction with the Communist party continues, Breton and the Surrealists sign with some Communist members, political declarations (such as the statement of the hundred and one intellectuals for Algerian independence). During the life of Breton, and after his death, the Surrealists never cease to speak out for various liberal causes; the tone of their periodicals, *Médium, Le Surréalisme, même, La Brêche,* and *Archibras,* is not at all unlike that of *La Révolution surréaliste.* At the end of his life, Breton, enfeebled, suffering badly from asthma, entrusts the leadership of the group to some of the young Surrealists. Two months before his death, a ten-day meeting of the Surrealist group and several commentators of Surrealism is held in Normandy (at Cerisy-la-Salle). Although Breton is supposed to have taken a great interest in it, he is unable to come, but the vociferous and enthusiastic disputes there prove that Surrealism has lost none of its energy. During the 1968 May-June events in France, the Surrealists take a position far more revolutionary than that of the French Communist party (see the special number of *Archibras* for the occasion). Breton would not have disapproved.

II   *Breton and Others*

On one point, closely related to the remarks above, the completely opposed views of Breton's critics are especially interesting —that is, his attitude toward youth. Breton was until the moment of his death eager to show his appreciation of the new, of the young, of the revolutionary. Claude Mauriac, son of the famous Catholic novelist, accuses him of having favored the most imitative and most pathetic manifestations from a real fear of underestimating any human possibilities. Breton the critic, says Mauriac along with a number of others, went beyond what he knew and even beyond what he genuinely thought. "Having been in the avant-garde, and having been unanimously recognized· for its leader, he never stopped being afraid that he might be left behind. Whence his inconceivable indulgence in the face of the most frivolous attempts of an untalented youth, to whom he always tends to give credit, just because it is youth and because it claims to be revolutionary." [2]

And on the other side, Victor Crastre contends that Breton's generosity to movements and persons which might have gone beyond Surrealism in some way should be seen as of primary importance. Referring to one of the passages where Breton claims that he would be the first to desert Surrealism if he found it to lag behind in relation to some other current of thought, Crastre remarks: "I am not a Surrealist, Breton would say at the very moment when his attitude would be the most Surrealist attitude imaginable." [3]

No judgments of this sort will be made in the following pages. That Breton was generous toward others when he ought perhaps not to have been, that he was at other times perhaps wrongly ungenerous—different readers will find these things touching, understandable, unforgivable, depending mainly on their attitude toward Breton as a person. Because of his lifelong identification with the movement which he founded and led, he is discussed here less as an individual than as a Surrealist author, and then not only as an author but as the spokesman for the Surrealist situation. There again, I think he would not have disapproved.

CHAPTER 2

Andre Breton and Surrealism

Plus tard vous apprendrez qui nous sommes (Later on you will learn who we are). "Ligne brisée," *Le Revolver à cheveux blancs*

I *The Moment and the Group*

Breton says of his own "very sinuous path" that it

passes through Heraclitus, Abelard, Eckhardt, Retz, Rousseau, Swift, Sade, Lewis, Arnim, Lautréamont, Engels, Jarry, and some others. I have made for myself a system of coordinates, a system which has withstood my personal experiences and therefore seems to me to include some chances for tomorrow. (*Manifestes,* p. 342)[1]

To this catalogue of mysticism, alchemy, antibourgeois revolution, black humor, eroticism, and reliance on the play of contraries, all elements which are easily discerned in Surrealist works in general and in Breton's work in particular, it is easy to add Freud (with the restrictions discussed later) and the importance of the unconscious, Hegel and the dialectical process as well as the idea of the hegemony of poetry over the arts, Rimbaud and the disorientation of the senses as well as the "anguishing" split between the self speaking and the other self, and the importance to be placed on language as evocation and incantation. Of course, at certain moments, the occult takes precedence over the theoretical ideal, just as in the early days of Surrealism the emphasis falls on automatic processes for transcribing the relevations of the unconscious while in later periods Breton laments the history of automatism as a regrettable series of misfortunes. What the public or the critic sees as inconsistency may be just that, or it may be a misinterpretation, or a failure to understand the premise from the beginning, or merely the effect of looking at one side of the alternation of dualities instead of at both. All this does not matter to the Surrealist in any case: if the fault is with the critic, then it simply shows the futility of endeavoring to judge from the outside. "I proclaim in this matter the right to absolute severity. No concessions to the world and no forgiveness. *With the terrible bargain in our hands*" (*Manifestes* p. 21). If the fault is with the "history" of past Surrealist attitudes, then it only proves the necessity of relying on the present moment rather than on past commitment: "Each full moment carries within itself the negation of centuries of limping and broken history" (*Manifestes,* p. 343).

In addition to the names already cited, that of Marx should be mentioned as another of the obvious allegiances of Breton; the reasons for all these lines of allegiance are clear. The act of reinterpreting the work must be linked to the activity of transmuting the world, to use the alchemical term to which Breton was so attached. Or, as he puts it: " 'Transform the world," said Marx; 'change life,' said Rimbaud: these two goals make only one for us" (*Manifestes,* p. 285).

All the Surrealists quote Lautréamont's statement that poetry must be made by all (and, adds Breton, it must be heard by all, although this point is one on which the attitude differs, as has already been obvious—it depends on the *moment*).[2] Their work is at all times a work in common, their attitude is the attitude of a group, implying as that does, certain peculiar strengths and other peculiar weaknesses. For instance, on the positive side, their cooperation in creations which could not have been the result of one brain alone, in metaphors whose *valeur secouante,* or disturbing content, depends on their multiple origin (see the preface to *Le Cadavre exquis,* a 1948 exhibition of folded-paper drawings produced by the playing of a game). On the negative side, the severity of discipline and the clash of personalities was (and still is) responsible for difficulties which do not always involve only the theory of Surrealism. Members are exiled (Artaud, Desnos), hard feelings are generated (Aragon, Breton), then ex-members are forgiven (see Breton's remarks on Tzara and on Desnos) and then different, or the same members leave the group for political reasons (Tzara, Eluard); and all of this one can read in any of the numerous histories of Surrealism.

II *Politics*

Two things must still be said, or rather, touched on, in what
concerns Surrealism as a whole. First the history of its relations
with the Marxist revolution of class struggle; in the early 1930's,
the Surrealists allied themselves for a time with the Communists,
in the hope of a definite conciliation between the two movements,
the two "revolutions." But various irritations occurred. Breton
publicly defended an anarchistic poem of Aragon ("Le Front
rouge") as poetry, therefore not to be taken seriously on a
political level: see the pamphlet *Misère de la poésie*. Under pressure (according to some historians), Aragon, having just returned
from the Soviet Union, renounced Breton's defense of him and
split off from the Surrealists. The repercussions were great, protests
on one side or the other came in from all over the world, insisting
that the "content" of a poem be restricted to the realm of poetry,
or refusing to relegate it *only* to that realm. That Breton himself
was assigned to a cell of gas workers and given the dullest sort
of work to do seems to indicate that the French Communist party
was never to have great faith in the Surrealists, whose allegiance
was, so it appeared to them, more to a poetic attitude than to a
practical commitment. After 1935, the Surrealists broke with
the Communists, retaining, however, their strong Marxist inclina-
tions and fervent admiration for Trotsky, whom Breton joined in
Mexico and with whom he wrote a manifesto concerning the
freedom of art. Although the Surrealists and the Communists have
at times taken the same positions, there remains a good deal of
animosity between them. At the time of the May 1968 student
and worker uprising in France, the present group of Surrealists
wrote vituperative manifestoes against the "nonrevolutionary"
attitude of the Communist party.

If one follows Breton's own remarks on the subject, his attitude
is perfectly clear and perfectly consistent. For him, it is essential
that man be in permanent revolt against limits of all kinds. To
accept as a goal of revolution a specific condition (such as the
overthrowing of a class or the furnishing of satisfactory material
benefits to all men) is to limit that revolution, to set a possible
term on it. At various times he and the other Surrealists also
protest against the *use* of art for "propaganda" (not only on one

side, but on any side, including the "good" side: see Benjamin Péret's *Le Déshonneur des poètes,* an attack on a volume of Resistance poetry called *L'Honneur des poètes).* Art cannot be used, it must be free and here Breton quotes the young Marx on the necessary liberty of the pen. Freedom of the mind is, from the Surrealist point of view, even more important than freedom from hunger. Nevertheless, in the alternations which characterize Surrealism, Breton insists that any painting must hold its own in front of a world of famine, must bear juxtaposition with the greatest human suffering if it is to be worth anything at all.

"Existence is elsewhere." Nothing matters if it is not the "annihilation of being in a *blind and interior diamond."* This distance once placed between Surrealists and their world, between the exterior, whatever appearance it may have, and the interior brilliance, may seem later to have been almost abolished; but to some extent its effect is always present. The alchemical process to which the poetic process is so often compared, is literally devoted to the producing of the interior diamond. The alternations between the attitudes of poetry-for-all and of prevent-the-public-from-entering have already been mentioned: the difficulty lies very deep, far too deep for anyone not connected with the movement to do more than mention it.

"My present feeling": Breton, the acknowledged leader of the group until his death, and the man whose spirit is alive among them still, provides the most interesting center for a study of Surrealism. Many of the clearest *documents* of these attitudes seen through his eyes are not discussed here,[3] precisely because they are documents or discourses and as such do not fall into the neat and arbitrary "formal" divisions chosen: *Entretiens,* or a series of interviews over the years 1913–1952, "Position politique de l'art aujourd'hui," "Discours au congrès des écrivains," and so on.

III *Art*

The final point has to do with the notion of art. The Dada movement, with which Breton was allied before the formation of the Surrealist group, is considered to have *only* made fun of art, although the Dada essays on poetry and on visual art written by Tristan Tzara, the guiding spirit of the movement, are in reality just as positive as they are negative.[4] "Art is liquidating itself as are countries," says Breton in an early Dada essay ("Distances," *Les Pas perdus,* p. 55). But in Surrealism, poetry is never to be attacked, only the "art" of prose. All Surrealist work is, from the point of view of its content, poetic, since the Surrealist attitude is identified by the Surrealists themselves with the poetic or "lyric" attitude. That is the essential connecting link between all these arbitrary divisions in this book, as unimportant in themselves as the variations of weather and of time.

Poetry is an attitude, not a form. Prose depreciates the world, and language; poetry exhilarates both. Surrealism, whatever framework it takes, goes beyond that framework to the space of poetry.

CHAPTER 3

Word and Image: *"a la lumiere de l'image"*

Cet été les roses sont bleues; le bois c'est du verre. (This summer the roses are blue; the wood is glass, *Premier Manifeste,* p. 63).

From the beginning, Surrealism as conceived by Breton was a totally uncompromising movement. The positions taken and the theories stated all had a remarkable quality of certainty and of a highly moral commitment. When members were excluded, the reason given was usually that they had in some way compromised, either with journalism (as in the case of Robert Desnos), with bourgeois society (as in the case of Antonin Artaud, of whom Breton says that he will always remember him "with policemen on either side"), or with public favor (in the case of Max Ernst, who accepted a PRIZE, considered by the Surrealists a complete indignity and a betrayal of Surrealist purity). Breton remained faithful to an image of himself as revolutionary and of Surrealism as a total and permanent revolt against accepted judgments and habits. Through the most obvious inconsistencies, this fidelity lends an undeniable unity to all his work.

I   Premier manifeste

Even at the outset of the first manifesto the invocation Breton addresses to the imagination, when he is describing man as a dreamer (*"ce rêveur définitif"*) and the dream as the center of the *real* Surrealist life, is based on the imagination's *unforgiving* quality: "Beloved imagination, what I cherish above all in you is that you never pardon." Relentless, *entier*, the Surrealist spirit has in its great intensity no room for the ordinary patterns of mediocre life, where it is thought necessary to adapt in order to "get along."

The man who is honestly able to echo Breton's famous credo about the possible reconciliation of the apparently contradictory states of dreams and reality—"I believe in the future resolution of these two states"—has no patience with any *adjustment* between ordinary states or conditions and beliefs. He is firmly rooted in the future and in the space which imagination creates beyond the borders of everyday life. Obviously, Surrealism should not be "treated" like any other literary movement, which has its period of influence between such and such years, in such and such a location. It considers itself to be on a different level from ordinary or traditional concerns, no matter how metaphysical they may be. It is a hand pointing away from all that we already know. In this first manifesto, Breton protests the efforts of the human imagination to "bring the unknown back to the known," to reduce all we find difficult to understand to the most easily understood basis; the manifesto ends with the haughty proclamation: "Existence is elsewhere."

As one would expect, the bourgeois standards of art are found lacking in the same criteria as are the logical standards of thought and expression. Not only are they dull and uninteresting in themselves, but they succeed in reducing all they judge to the same dullness, constantly satisfactory to the majority who need to be reassured, and therefore abhorrent to the Surrealist revolutionaries. Good taste, as a flattening of the individual instinct, is to be challenged whenever possible: "In the bad taste of my time, I try to go further than anyone else." (It is to be noticed here that Breton is never content to go only *as far as* anyone else, which would be an essentially traditional attitude. His choice of bad taste as a provocative gesture would have been substantially undercut by such a willingness to seem, even in a minor way, even in a detail of style, like even a few others.) Good taste is usually thought of as that which does not "stand out"; in contrast, the scenery and the objects valued by the Surrealists have an extreme quality, a remarkable oddness (in the sense that one notices them)—the Gothic novel (*"roman noir"*), the scenery of ruins and ruined castles, and the whole series of mannequins, masks, personal eccentricities, and the like. Many of these show a certain morbid fascination not with the cruel and the unreal alone but with the denial of life and movement. And in fact, it would be interesting from this point of view to compare them with several of Breton's favorite images, such as a locomotive going full speed suddenly stopped in an overgrown forest, or a group of highly sophisticated

machines dropped into water which will paralyze them, both
images revealing the same cruelty toward *regular* motion and the
same exaltation of the bizarre or irregular cessation of the motion.
   Breton eulogizes the *insolite* or the unexpected, the spontaneously revealed marvelous in the pattern of repetitions and cres-
cendo which is typical of the most forceful Surrealist statements:
"The marvelous is always beautiful, nothing but the marvelous is
beautiful" (*Manifestes,* p. 27). The fact that the *merveilleux* is
rare prevents the "always" from imposing a stifling custom on the
"esthetic" principle, which is enunciated and then extended to
convince the reader that all forms of the marvelous are valuable,
even those generally thought hideous or even trivial. The latter is,
of course, far harder to accept, since most readers of Breton are
familiar enough with nineteenth-century writers to have already
encountered and even *approved* the theory of the grotesque as
esthetically important. (It is, needless to say, never the case that
Breton simply repeats already familiar principles.) And the
third part of the repetition effectively shuts out all customary
definitions of beauty with an uncompromising finality.
   His attack on the traditional passages of description in the
novel, for which he takes as an example the depiction of a room
in Dostoevski's *Crime and Punishment,* depends on a refusal to
liken people to other people—that is, to reduce them—or individual experiences and esthetic judgments to other experiences
and judgments, or the emotions of one person to emotions of
another, or even to the other emotions of the same individual:
"I have too unstable a notion of the continuity of life to equal to
my best moments my moments of depression, of weakness" (p.
20). Of course this is tantamount to blatantly advocating a certain separation between art and life, since he would deprive the
former of any trace of the "worthless moments" along with the
weak and depressing ones. What is unworthy of being crystallized
in permanent form will eventually disappear from the perfect
Surrealist universe.
   But such uncompromising attitudes will raise a difficulty in the
matter of automatic transcription which Breton emphasizes at this
point as the basic process of Surrealism: "Pure psychic automatism by means of which it is hoped to express . . . the real
functioning of thought. Dictation of thought, in the absence of

any control exerted by reason, outside of all esthetic and moral preoccupation" (p. 40). Surrealism is an act of faith in the superior reality of certain forms of mental association and of the dream, both understood as totally free of any of the constraints that logic, ethics, or esthetic judgment usually impose.

Now if the unconscious should happen to dictate a dull ordinary description of a room closely resembling that described in *Crime and Punishment,* what would be the reaction of the Surrealist? Breton states quite clearly that he believes in the infallibility of his own thought, that "thought is strong, and incapable of being in error." Any weakness it shows is the result of exterior distractions, never of the "interior" inspiration, which is supposed to be so reliable that any stylistically weak sentence in the "dictation" will be immediately balanced by the strength of the sentence following it. Breton finds the appeal of inspiration so overwhelming that he likens it to a drug, calling the "spoken thought" technique (*"la pensée parlée"*) inescapable once one has experienced it. It is impossible to leave Surrealism of one's own accord, exactly as if it were a habit dangerous to acquire. All the statements about Surrealism contribute to this view; just the image of man *soluble* in his thought, one of Breton's favorites, is enough to put off the weak-hearted inquirer. One sometimes wonders if Breton deliberately accentuates this extreme side of the experiments because of having felt himself without it to be somewhat of an *ennuyeux:* "as far as I am concerned, I used to be considered as tedious as rain—I still am" (p. 33).

But Breton takes pains to point out that his elder, Pierre Reverdy, was "at least as boring" as he is, just before quoting Reverdy's famous description of the image as the "bringing together of two more or less distant realities," whose force depends on the distance between the elements of the image as much as on the *"justesse"* of their relationship. Breton underlines the fact that Reverdy's esthetic is *a posteriori,* that it is a description or way of judging images already found instead of a recipe for discovering new images. The Surrealist does not invent images—rather he becomes aware of them when they force their way into his consciousness, as if they were knocking on a window pane. The Surrealist will eventually be compared to a medium, but never to a craftsman. In a "state of grace," or perfect receptivity, he receives the orders of the marvelous without ever contradicting them. (See Breton's "Lettre aux voyantes" of 1925 with its lament for the men forever "lost" for not having followed these orders as they came.)

In short, this primary manifesto is a testimony of wonder and acceptance in the face of the marvelous, accompanied by a declaration of absolute nonconformism in the face of the world. Social man in his waking state is held to be less authentic and more limited than man in his dreaming state; in fact, the waking state can be regarded as a tedious *interference* with the limitless domain of the dream.

II   Deuxième manifeste

The second manifesto carries still further the notion of non-compromise, preferably at the risk of social exclusions: "I insist on being considered extremist" (p. 168). "The public's approval is to be shunned above all. The public must be forbidden *to enter* if confusion is to be avoided. . . . SURREALISM MUST BE MADE PROFOUNDLY AND GENUINELY OCCULT" (p. 211). Again the tone is categorical, stubborn: *"Je tiens," "Il faut," "Je demande."* The demand is purposely pushed to the extreme, fortified with terms which banish any possibility of nuance: "fanatique," *"par-dessus tout," "absolument."* It is never a question of tactful omission for the purpose of public communication, of Surrealism simply withdrawing to an inner sanctum; Breton deliberately emphasizes the exclusion of the non-Surrealists by the terms *"empêcher d'entrer"* and *"l'occultation profonde véritable."* One would have thought the *hiding* of Surrealism sufficient, without the terms being reinforced by two others, both far stronger than the first. This particular technique, which could be described by an accumulation of intensity, fits the frequent personal portraits of Breton as a leonine figure of powerful attraction, given to extremes of enthusiasm and dismay, somehow living on a different level from ordinary mortals who are less violent in their alternations of mood and judgment. It is partly this intensity of feeling which convinces him (rightly) that he can speak to and be heard by all the young people who *refusent le pli,* that is, who will not be molded according to the worn-out ideas of family, country, and religion which it is the Surrealists' purpose to wreck, along with the related ideas of calm and happiness. If Surrealism calls itself the tail of Romanticism, the expression is appropriate precisely because of its repeated denunciations of the "stupid illusion" of contentment and harmony; if it insists on calling itself a very "prehensile" tail, that part of the expression is appropriate in its indication that Surrealism cannot be considered *only* a repetition of a former movement—it is that and more.

Anyone firmly attached to the bourgeois modes of existence or who cares about the place he occupies in the world (and here Breton italicizes the words *dans le monde* to convey his scorn for such an attitude) could not conceivably be alive to the multiplication of short circuits taking place in the Surrealist atmosphere. Surrealism is a "mental situation" (*"lieu mental"*), an activity of the mind (or, as Breton and Tzara called Dada, a "state of mind") mainly directed at the search for a particular *point de l'esprit* or *point sublime* from which all the contradictions we face will no longer be seen as contradictions. Death and life, past and future, real and imaginary, height and depth will communicate: the point is again a more extreme or dramatic image than the later and more tangible image of the communicating vessels (see *Les Vases communicants*) since the emphasis on the location and precision contrasts so markedly with the juxtaposed catalogue of contradictions. References to a "point sublime" recur in a great deal of Breton's writing, like the image of the *fil* or connecting thread, both clear expressions of the constant and solemn quest for an ideal unity behind all the series of dualities of which the Surrealists are so conscious.

Man is trapped in the already known, in the already thought— but as the unknown and the marvelous are allowed to penetrate the supposedly closed world of the known, the *thought* (*"le pensé"*) will gradually succumb to the *thinkable* (*"le pensable"*) in a universe at last open to imagination and to chance. But when the accepted logical fixity of the known gives way, an abyss of madness opens up beneath. Since there is nothing comfortable about following this road of the marvelous above the abyss, many choose a safer path: as Breton states in both the *Second Manifesto* and later in the *Prolegomena to a Third Manifesto or Not,* this more dangerous road cannot even be protected with railings (*"garde-fou"*). Such *fixed* protection would be itself a

threat to the newly open universe, which is admittedly a dangerous
one. When Breton wishes to praise Picasso, he calls him the artist
who places no railing on his bridges; this is a further example of
Surrealism's *"caractère entier,"* its uncompromising intensity.
Better to fall into madness (Breton gives a certain value to the fall
itself, as he states in another connection) or "to pass through to
the other side of the mirror" than not to dare the adventure. Surrealism, after all, exists to see and to show "the other side of the
real," and one can scarcely expect that to be a trivial vision.

Nor can the means of vision be trivial. Breton compares the
Surrealists' attitude toward their work with that of the alchemists—
the value of the philosopher's stone was that it permitted the
"dazzling revenge" of the human imagination on everything else.
He takes Rimbaud's term *l'alchimie du verbe* in its fullest sense,
the Word being the model for the human soul, the omnipresent
mover of the universe: "thus it is as much in what we fear as in
what we write, as in what we love." In opposition to all the dulling categories of ordinary life, the Surrealist work is a noble
crusade toward the limits of the human mind.[1] The *Second Manifesto* ends with an eloquent invocation to mental adventure, which
takes full account of the possibility of failure and determines to
count even that a victory:

Let him use in spite of all prohibitions, the avenging weapon of the
idea against the bestiality of all beings and of all things; and then
one day when he is vanquished—but vanquished only if the *world is
world*—let him greet the firing of the sad guns as if it were a salute.
(p. 221)

III   Prolégomènes à un troisième manifeste ou non

The *Prolegomena to a Third Manifesto of Surrealism or Not*
begin with Breton's disclaimer of a total adhesion to any system;
he explains that there is too much of the Northerner in him for
that, too much "granite" and "fog." As a balance to the hope and
pride represented by the possibility of a *point sublime,* he discerns
the possibility of a *point faillible* in all the theories he has held. No
system of principles is perfect, even alone or in its ideal state,
and in combination with human fallibility, the imperfect is ag-
gravated; "perhaps every great idea is liable to serious alteration
the moment it comes in contact with the mass of men, where it is

forced to compromise with minds of a different temper than those from which it sprang" (p. 338). There follows a negative catalogue; "As long as men have not become conscious of their condition . . . , it is not worth talking . . . it is still less worth loving . . . it is still less worth dying and . . . still less worth living." But directly preceding the last factor of this series is a lyrical parenthesis: "I always think of youth, of the trees *in bloom* in New York," which is echoed by the next sentence: *"There is,* I think of that beautiful optimistic formula of gratitude which recurs in Apollinaire's last poems . . ." (p. 340). This is the beginning of a totally positive catalogue balancing the negative one as the consciousness of a fallible point balances that of a sublime one—the style and the temper of Surrealism are to a great extent determined by the play of dualities and their alternating resolution and redivision.

And then Breton moves from the statement of the marvelous (*"Il y a": there is*) to the demands of humanism (*"Il faut": there must be*). Man must no longer be exploited by his fellow man, or by the "absurd and provocative idea" of God. The idea of love must also be reexamined, and finally, man must put himself forever "on the side of man." The passage builds up to a final series of impatient protests: "Enough weakness, enough childishness . . . enough flowers on graves, enough civic instruction between two classes of gym, enough tolerance, enough serpents!" (p. 341). The *opposition* must be strengthened; men must be convinced that when "everyone" has agreed on a thing, the only way out of the imprisoning *likeness* of belief is an individual resistance to the common perception. Breton calls the latter the only key to the fields (see *La Clé des champs*). He claims as the goal of his voyage to which he invites us "the opening of windows" on the greatest "utopian landscapes."

All Dada and Surrealist manifestations are manifestoes of liberation. When man explores his own subconscious, this exploration is supposed to free him from the constraints of society and art; when he commits himself to the Surrealist principles, it is not as if this were to be another reassuring category: Breton states plainly that there can be too much conformism even among the Surrealists. Surrealism is to be a continuing scandal (corresponding to the "scandal of the world") and a personal risk, or it will not be.

CHAPTER 4

Les Pas perdus (1917-1924)

I Freedom and Risk

The primary impulse for these essays, which cover the period of Dada through the separation of Tzara and the Surrealists, is once more the problem of freedom. "La Confession dédaigneuse" at the beginning of the collection is a haughty attack on the idea of human experience and *equilibrium,* that is, on man's instinctive assimilation or adaptation of things to himself and himself to things. Luckily, says Breton, the sense of equilibrium (or placidity) is disturbed when conditions no longer favor it, and this change of conditions is inevitable. The goal of the revolutionary artist or writer is to destroy, at least mentally, these conditions so as to liberate the human mind from this imprisoning self-satisfaction. Breton, twenty-seven years old, claims that he has not known such equilibrium for a long time, and that the same could be said of all those who share in his mental aristocracy, which is equivalent to a state of unrest (*"inquiétude"*). He, like his friends, refuses to adapt, to present a social face to social situations, to take comfort in any *belief,* because such "vulgar" compromise would betray the spirit of surrealism. The creed of these unadaptables is stated, categorically, on the first page of the essay:

Absolutely incapable of accepting the fate which is mine, stricken in my highest consciousness by the denial of justice which is, in my eyes, not in the least excused by original sin, I make an effort not to adapt my life to the ridiculous conditions of existence *here below* (p. 8).

The terms are, as always, extreme: *"absolument," "aucunement," "dérisoire,"* "ici-bas." The Dada revolution was supposed to be a highly moral revolution, as Tzara and the other Dadaists agree. It might have seemed a purely frivolous manifestation against the bourgeois culture and civilization to whose bankruptcy World War I bore witness, but it was profoundly moral in its deliberately scandalous attacks on all it found scandalous. It is in moral concerns that Breton feels he always found his "main subjects of exaltation." The passage from the absolute to the relative and from doubt to negation (here he quotes Barrès) must somehow be made without losing moral values. Consistency of thought or expression matters little, since inconsistency is an honest indication of the contradictions Breton finds everywhere in the human character and the human condition—these contradictions reflecting the inescapable dualities which he calls the "marvelous wound" revealed by Rimbaud (*"Caractère de l'évolution moderne"*).[1] What matters, and matters greatly, is the basic morality of the concern.

In this respect, the Dada/Surrealist conception of poetry goes even beyond philosophy in its *dépassement* of practical utility and far beyond the traditional concept of poetry in its effort to restore content to form. Breton insists, for instance, that Racine's moral dissertations are absolutely "unworthy of the admirable expression they adopt." For him, poetry is, in spite of all its disappointments, the place where the terrible conflicts of consciousness and confidence in the individual mind have the best chance of being solved. In poetic language the equivocal can be maintained, whereas the nature of prose makes it less hospitable to the expression of dualities, resolved or not. The notion of the *équivoque* is a positive counterpart of the abhorred idea of *équilibre*. If the balance is generative of a greater number of ideas, it is to be valued; but insofar as the balance of a greater number of ideas, it is to be valued; but insofar as the balance of ideas lends stability, it must be rejected in the interest of surrealist "vertige." In a discussion of Lautréamont's *Chants de Maldoror*,[2] Breton describes the exhilaration of holding two opposing ideas *"en ballottage,"* in a perfect state of indecision, where both can be tossed about without a betrayal of one side for the other, without reduction or simplification. The active play of alternates is akin to the basic notion of dialectic which appeals to Dadaists and Surrealists alike.[3] The alternation of opposites is often reflected in their preference for a style of paradox, a style to which poetry and "poetic" prose are particularly well suited. When Breton defends, in an extremely important passage of the essay "Clairement," his affection for poetry, he explains that in his interpretation of the word, it has more to do with the lives of writers (or nonwriters) than with what they write or could write. And the definition he gives shows as well as any other group of terms the paradoxical style: "the manner in which an individual seems to have accepted the unacceptable human condition" (p. 135).

This is their definition of poetry as well as of human life seen at its best: both are based on an extreme consciousness of the equivocal and of the necessity (and even the beauty) of the absurdities of the "real." In his "Confession dédaigneuse," Breton states his gratitude to Jacques Vaché[4] for having prevented him from being a *poet* in the traditional sense of the word. Poetry, for the Dadaists and the Surrealists, is a totally uncompromising attitude and never a pleasing series of words, or, even worse, rhymes. Poetry is, to take a lofty and yet typical example, Breton's refusal to be attached: "I used never to leave my house without having said a definite goodbye to everything that had occurred there in the way of tenacious[5] memories, to everything of myself I felt I might perpetrate there" (p. 12). Poetry is the love of the unfinished, of things unaccomplished. Taking the opposite point of view from Montaigne, who said that man embraces too much and so ends up with nothing,[6] Breton answers that his goal is more than anything else that of embracing everything. Poetry is the willingness to risk, *foolishly,* all the comfortable situations for a simple shadow and then to call the risk justified: "and it is enough, for the moment, that such a lovely shadow dances on the sill of the window out of which I will begin to jump every day again" (p. 24). *"Je vais recommencer chaque jour":* the reference to the future and to the repeated future of the act emphasizes the promise and the frequency of the risk, while the sufficiency of the reward stated at the beginning contrasts with the shadowy reward itself and the extremity of the risk at the very end.

Breton's criticism of the Dada movement is based exactly on the minimum consequences of the risk. He complains in "Lâchez tout" that Dada was for some a way out, a way not of adventuring but of sitting down. That the movement should have ended not by a revolution, but in the windows of bookstores and in café discussions, is a terrible disappointment. He laments the extraordinary disproportion between the revolution in ideas and its negligible consequences in the world. Dada was a stranger to dialectic, and thus unaware of the essential connection between the inner activity of ideas and their outer results. The final ad-

monition of Breton to his followers in the mental aristocracy of
adventure is justly famous:

> Leave everything.
> Leave Dada.
> Leave your wife, leave your mistress.
> Leave your hopes and your fears.
> Sow your children in the corner of a forest.
> Leave the prey for the shadow.
> Leave, if need be, an easy life and all you are given
>   for a possible situation in the future.
> Set out on the highways. (p. 132)

Dada was useful to the Surrealists only as a way of keeping
themselves unattached to anything, in a state of perfect *"disponibilité,"* as Breton explains in "Clairement"; a retrospective
statement, this is in no way contradicted by the attitude of the
future Surrealists at the moment of their greatest enthusiasm for
Dada. The opening paragraph of Breton's own essay "Pour Dada"
is a protest against all limits imposed by mental habits and happenings exterior to him:

It is impossible for me to conceive of a joy of the mind in any other
·way than as a call to freedom. How could it be at ease within the
limits which almost all books, almost all events, impose upon it? I
doubt there is any man who has not felt, at least once in his life, the
temptation to deny the exterior world. (p. 85)

Dada signified freedom not only from usual customs and bourgeois judgments, but also from all the imprisonments of logic and
literature seen as *work*. "Pour Dada" reads as a celebration of the
spontaneously created images (which Breton calls *"trouvailles"*
or found things, connecting them to the old-fashioned term "inspiration" that he would like to put back into use). The notions
of the innocent and the arbitrary stressed in this essay are also
linked to the notion of freedom, since innocence implies the absence or denial of any previous knowledge or experience which
might weigh down the mind. He puts an equal stress on the arbitrary, since chance implies the absence or denial of logical
progression and order. Those who are sufficiently innocent to
accept the arbitrary as a guide for living and writing have come
to the realization that "nothing is so serious, so definitive." After

such a realization, it is possible, as Breton admits, for a man to place himself again under the "common law," that is, to compromise once more with the experiences and logic of the outside world. But some do not, and they risk everything. "Those who have paid for this marvelous minute of lucidity by being permanently disturbed continue to be called poets: Lautréamont, Rimbaud, but to tell the truth, literary childishness stopped with them" (p. 85). Poetry as writing or living is no longer to be played with—a new terrorism, as Breton puts it, makes that impossible.

II *Doubt*

Breton's "Deux manifestes dada" contain terse and convincing descriptions of Dada "as a state of mind" in which all the former kinds of language are suddenly felt to be unworkable. This is only partly the deliberate choice of ambiguity and contradiction ("You have only to pronounce a sentence for the opposite sentence to become Dada"); it is more significantly a genuine realization of the psychological discrepancy between the speaker's wishes and his words ("I have seen Tristan Tzara without any words to order a pack of cigarettes in a tobacco shop"; "You can know the word 'hello' perfectly well and say 'goodbye' to the woman you find again after a year's absence"). Language is the worst convention of all, and it is chiefly in our attack upon it that we are poets.

The terrain Dada chooses for its manifestations is the terrain of *doubt;* unfortunately, it is not always possible to limit the precise boundaries chosen, or to prevent the doubt from turning against the person who uses it. The easier counterpart of doubt is the provocation of others. For Dada, provocation is always more valuable than acceptance, the shock of any statement contributing in large measure to its vitality. "A true saying will always profit by taking an outrageous form of expression," says Breton in a speech of 1922 in Barcelona on the "Caractères de l'évolution moderne et ce qui en participe." Unfortunately, the provocation wears off rapidly. In our present cultural climate one cannot conceive any longer of a *"poésie maudite,"* because everyone immediately accepts the most outlandish sentiments as one more cultural phenomenon; once the absorption process of the larger culture starts, the originality of the protest vanishes in a common approval. Even

though the writer of revolutionary tracts leaves no margins at the
side of his pages or in his mind—and Breton makes a point of
saying that he leaves none—still the text will be watered down by
the well-meaning public, always parasitic on the ideas of a few.
Many of the metaphors used by the Dadaists and Surrealists are
metaphors of violence, such as Breton's famous remark that the
simplest Surrealist act would be to go down in the street and fire
on the first passerby. And their attacks on the traditional places
of culture are extreme: they call the museum where certain art
objects are *consecrated* a place of entombment[7] and recommend
instead the unplanned living performance of the streets or the
planned and insulting performance of desecration. Of course, the
same recommendation extends to educational institutions—for
example, the Surrealist Robert Desnos calls for all amphitheaters
(representing the imparting of traditional knowledge under traditional forms) to be deserted for the new adventure of the streets.
Yet this is not sufficient as a permanent revolt. Historians of art
hold exhibitions of Dada and Surrealist art within the museums
themselves, and amphitheaters are eventually used for lectures on
Dada and Surrealism. Breton foresees this ultimate danger very
clearly; in the essay "Distances" he laments the fact that even the
notion of *"inequiétude"* (unrest, mental discomfort) has become
a system.

While endeavoring not to "slip on the parquet floor of sentimentality (*"Après Dada"*) and not to permit Surrealism to make
of itself a systematic structure (an accusation often leveled, which
Breton always denied), Breton does nevertheless express a continuing faith in the *idea* as a generative force. He takes a position
contrary to that of Picabia ("One must be a nomad," said Picabia,
"crossing ideas as one crosses countries or towns") and maintains that, even if the risk is a silly one, "even if all the ideas
should be such as to disappoint us, I intend nonetheless from the
beginning to devote my life to them" (p. 127). Dada is usually
said to have committed suicide in 1922 as a final negative or
"pure" act (which justifies Breton's title *"Après dada"*), although
Tzara refuses up to the end of his life to separate his early writings
from his later ones by calling some "pre-Dada" and some "post-
Dada." Dada was to him a continuing process; and Surrealism
considers itself a continuing quest: "Perhaps 'the place and the

formula' will always escape me, but it can never be repeated
enough that it is a matter of the search for the theme more than
anything else" (p. 126).

III   Art and Language

Art is, for the Surrealists, a way of knowledge. Painting is useless insofar as it represents, useless when it tells us what we already
know, and never valuable on purely esthetic grounds:

I persist in thinking that a painting or a sculpture can be envisaged
only secondarily as an object of taste and can be justified only insofar
as it is able to advance by at least one step what is properly called
our abstract knowledge. (p. 174)

In the essay "Distances," Breton bitterly denounces speculation in
the art market as the most definite and least defensible absorption
of revolution. But much of the blame falls on the individual artist
in his frequent misconception of the role of art. His ambition
should lie in another realm altogether from that of Renoir, who
could call the painting of a nude finished the moment he wanted
to give its bottom a spank. Surely there are more interesting revelations to be gained from art than that, says Breton, and he concludes ironically:

Let me just say that if we had undergone one influence rather than
another, we might not be where we are today: perhaps we would eat
fewer apples and perhaps we would not have to put up with the
proximity of that woman whom, since we did not invite her, we are
sick of finding stretched out on our sofas in more or less suggestive
poses. (p. 178)

All the Surrealist creates should, then, be the exact opposite
of the representational painting of such artists as Cézanne and
Renoir. Indeed, the two most important essays in this volume
on what was to be called Surrealist writing (in homage to Apollinaire, although not to his "reactionary" play Les Mamelles de
Tirésias),[8] make plain the enormous difference between the two
conceptions of art. Nor should the Surrealist permit himself to be
seduced by the temptation of the lesson into writing a novel with

a thesis, a play with a thesis, and so on. Marcel Duchamp is to be admired for his *"dédain de la thèse"* (scorn of a thesis) as well as for his effective destruction of what Breton calls the "lyricism-blackmail of a ready-made expression." When Duchamp signs a manufactured object as if it were his own work, when he bases all his decisions on a flip of the coin, his elevation of chance to the role art has been accustomed to play, it is the most powerful revenge that could be taken on the accepted esthetics. It is interesting, though not often mentioned, that Breton issues a definite warning at this juncture about not falling into a new mystique of art. The fact that the first wave of enthusiasm about automatic writing eventually subsides for the Surrealists does not imply a betrayal of what Surrealism once "stood for"; it is instead a testimony of Breton's fidelity to his own guiding principle.

But there is no doubt about the original enthusiasm. "Entrée des médiums" describes the sense which Breton and his friends give to Surrealism as a psychic automatism which corresponds to the "state of dreaming," a state which he first illustrates in terms of his personal experience. Just before going to sleep, phrases or sentences with no obvious meaning would present themselves to his mind, and he judged these to be "poetic elements of the first order." He and Philippe Soupault were able to reproduce in themselves at will the necessary state of abstraction from the outside world in order to receive these "magic dictations" which came at such speed that they had to take notes in shorthand in order not to lose any of the words. *Les Champs magnétiques* was the result of their efforts, each chapter being the simple recital of one day's dictation. Here Breton explains the risk haunting this exercise of the unconscious. One is endlessly and "maliciously" tempted to heed another voice besides that of the genuine unconscious, to change in some fashion, for *exterior* reasons (such as the esthetic or the logical) the dictates of the first voice which should be "sufficient unto itself." Any change is a compromise, and all compromise is fatal to the spirit of Surrealism. In spite of feeling that this dictation could not be *used* for any specific purpose, Breton is persuaded at this point and for a long time to come "that nothing that is said or done is worth anything" unless it is said or done under the orders of the unconscious. The more conscious elements enter into a creation and are thereby placed under the law of a human will-to-literature, the less fruitful will be any discoveries and revelations forthcoming from the creation.

The second illustration Breton gives in this essay is that of his friends' attempts to capture the language of the unconscious in the *"récit de rêves"* or recounting of dreams. But to the extent that the human memory is both limited and untrustworthy, the experiment has a built-in limit of usefulness. The documents produced were neither numerous nor characteristic.

The third kind of experience, however, is found to be so remarkable that, to use Breton's dramatic but not insincere terms, "the most blasé among us, the most sure of themselves, are taken aback, tremble with gratitude and fear; it might be said that they have lost countenance before the marvel." Under the instruction of a medium, René Crevel had learned to put himself to sleep and in this state was able to speak in a more or less flowing discourse, a procedure subsequently attempted by the other Surrealists. But even before describing these hypnotic sleep experiments, Breton is careful to say that the Surrealists have never taken the "spiritualistic" attitude and that he refuses any possibility of communication between the living and the dead. One might wonder why he should bother to stress that particular point, since few people are in danger of confusing spiritualism with Surrealism; but in any case the distinction he draws continues to hold, even when the Surrealists insist on the priority of sensations over ideas. (Breton claims that the reason for which he writes poetry is to re-create within himself the emotions or *sensations* he feels upon reading or experiencing certain things, stating in his "Caractères de l'evolution moderne . . . " that sensations have always been of primary importance to him, although they have never been of the "mystical" type.) [9]

Breton recounts in some detail the first experiences with sleep-writing. Desnos having expressed the greatest doubt about his own capacity for such experiments, and having recently exposed two public hypnotists himself, suddenly drops his head on his arm and scratches the table convulsively, then wakes up convinced that nothing unusual has transpired. The next day when the experience is repeated, he writes, answers questions, draws pictures, even though he is ordinarily unable to draw. Not all the group are successful at this: the essays end with a perfectly straightforward

remark by Breton that he, Paul Eluard, Max Ernst, and Max
Morise were never able to fall asleep under these conditions,
although they would have wished to do so. That Breton should be
so genuinely enthusiastic about an experiment in which he could
not himself participate is a testimony to his essential generosity
of spirit. Some may find it more indicative of his credulity, just as
one may suspect that Desnos and the others were occasionally
prone to exaggerate and overdramatize in order to win Breton's
full approval.[10]

The often-quoted essay "Les Mots sans rides" is a convincing
meditation on the newly discovered power of language and on the
responsibility of the poet toward it. Words must no longer be
considered simple and trustworthy auxiliaries to human thought—
it is time for their liberation. To succeed the verbal alchemy
Rimbaud spoke of, Breton calls for a verbal chemistry to bring into
existence all the possible meanings by scientific procedures. The
word must be regarded as independent in itself and in its new
relations with other words, the most refraining from attributing to
them the properties he would before have assumed they had. The
wrinkles shed by the words which are now rejuvenated as they are
set free from their long past resemble the "pleats" in Breton's
image of the young people who refuse *"le pli";* they are both
symptoms of fixity, the enemy of all new movements. Out of their
past grooves, words are suddenly weapons of the present and the
future. Now language recovers its original purpose, that of "ad-
vancing knowledge, of exalting life . . ." (p. 167). Equivalent to
art in its contribution to the most genuine form of learning, poetic
language intensifies and broadens the scope of life. Natural human
conservatism in its horror of infinite freedom would impose a
limitation and a dulling on linguistic experience, as on all other
kinds; to this end it insists that well-groomed speech take into
account before anything else the etymology of the word ("its
deadest weight," says Breton) so that all the vibrations of meaning
can be confined to a narrow range of order. The opposite of this
attitude is called poetry.

When for the first time a specific color was assigned to each
vowel sound (as in Rimbaud's "Sonnet à couleurs"), the word was
diverted from its "duty" to signify, so that it could be born into a
concrete, "architectural" existence.[11] The idea of freshness makes

a paradoxical contrast with the idea of verbal "innocence" on which Breton claims we can no longer count. He means, of course, that we as users of language cannot now rely on the submission of language to us and to our preconceived ideas: "What matters is that the alarm has been given and that from now on it seems imprudent to speculate on the innocence of words" (p. 168). All the melodramatic images here ("alarm," implying danger as does the term "imprudent," "innocence" implying the opposite, crime) and in the following sentences ("insufficient surveillance," "caught in the act") link this passage in tone to the highly dramatic "Entrée des médiums." Breton, who writes in such a lofty and elegant fashion himself, cares desperately about language: it is worth a certain amount of dramatic emphasis.

Words are the most effective creators of energy. They command thought itself, to which they give all its momentum. To the word plays at which Desnos excelled when "asleep" no trivial sense should be assigned; the essay ends with the celebrated lines:

> And let everyone understand that we say "play on words" when it is our deepest justifications which are in play. Besides, the words have finished playing.
> The words are making love. (p. 171)

CHAPTER 5

Point du Jour (1924-34)

The essays grouped under the title "Daybreak" include many of the major themes and theories of Surrealism, which could be placed in three general divisions—first, the role of language as a determiner of the world; second, the value of the unknown in contrast to the known, and of the multiple and equivocal in contrast to the simple; and finally, the connection between a certain contemporary state of unrest common to human beings and things on one hand and the miraculous revelation of a new "crystalline" reality on the other. The themes are at once inextricably linked and inseparable, both developing and unchanging over the decade covered in the essays, as is appropriate to the always paradoxical nature of Surrealism.

I *Reality and the Seer*

The "reality" in the title "Introduction au Discours sur le peu de réalité" is seen as "little" in quantity or minor in power in relation to the power of the human mind and of its weapon, the word. In this sense, the essay with this title which opens the collection is a continuation of the essay "Les Mots sans rides" of *Les Pas perdus*. Since, for Breton, no concrete reality exists outside of the individual, it is up to us to use all the methods we can devise to make the reality conform to what we would choose for it, or at least to rearrange its composition from time to time in order to avoid the stagnant immobility fatal to new thoughts and patterns of life. In the rearrangements of the world our most effective tool is language: what we say controls even what we are able to see.

"Doesn't the mediocrity of our universe depend essentially on our power of enunciation?" (p. 25). If we permit our words always to be reassembled in their ordinary ways, we are necessarily accepting the unchanging aspect of things as they have always appeared to

us. "Words tend to group themselves according to particular
affinities, with the general effect of recreating the world at every
moment according to the old model" (p. 24); there can be no new
vision without a new tongue.

The most frequent and the gravest mistake nonpoets make is to
"translate" poetic images into common terms under the excuse of
explaining them, a process which immediately does away with all
their potentially generative force. Against someone who tries to
explain that the poet Saint-Pol-Roux's image *"mamelle de cristal"*
(crystal breast) really means a vase, Breton unleashes a righteous
anger. One image does not *mean* another, and anyone who tries to
facilitate the task of the reader is actually reducing the priceless
complexity of the human imagination. "What is the point of this
will to reduce, this terror of what someone before me has called
the devil Plural?" (p. 21). Our love of simplicity leads us to
formulate easy categories; when we put things in a placid and satisfactory order, we are denying their capacity for multiplicity and
movement, and our own flexibility and range of vision. Surrealism
demands always the most complete experience, and often it insists
that this experience be shared by the greatest number.[1] Breton
claims the absolute equality of all men in front of the marvelous
dictation and the white page on which everything is already written
("Le Message automatique," p. 42). When he emphasizes the
Surrealist preference for the verbal images over purely visual ones,
he is of course speaking for the writers and not the painters; but
the reason he gives for the preference is the greater *richness* of
images which are verbally grasped. All the mannered effort of
"talented" writers is unfruitful compared with the extraordinary
profusion of images, "visual sensations," and expression granted
to the poet who is able to receive the dictation in a "state
of grace." All the labored attempts at describing "Baudelairean
correspondences" are already out of date, timid as they are in
comparison to the "dream values" which are the only values recognized by the Surrealists. Pointing to other images in an endless
sequence, Surrealist images are never frozen into a "perfect" poem
or into any other rigid framework. A passage of the essay "Exposition X . . ., Y" accuses the man incapable of perceiving these
images (such as a horse galloping on a tomato) of being an absolute idiot, calls the traditional poetic simile feeble, and implies by

its casual ending and absence of any effort to persuade that the man who does not instantly accept this simple statement of all the multiple metamorphoses within the Surrealist vision is just as much of an idiot.

> A tomato is also a child's balloon,
> Surrealism—I repeat—having suppressed
> the word "like." The horse is about to
> become one with the cloud, et cetera. (pp. 73-74)

In his "Introduction aux 'Contes Bizarres' d'Achim d'Arnim" Breton expands on the topic of the voluntary hallucination, on the making of oneself a seer in Rimbaud's sense, and on the extremely troubling effect such vision has on the notion of personality. As the exterior world undergoes from our point of view a change in appearance related to the more general "crisis of the object" which Breton finds characteristic of our time, as our doubt of accepted categories affects us in our turn, we are fated to undergo a crisis of personality. The contrary feelings of *"dédoublement"* (or the sense of double identity) and the loss of any personal identity ("where the notion of the *I* is shaken") exist side by side in the Surrealist believer. It is not only words which must be removed from their accustomed meanings and thus from their usual applications in deliberate *détournements*—the poet himself must be separated from all his accustomed settings and roots so that he becomes *dépaysé* (bewildered, and out of his element).

Moreover, Surreality will be a function of our willingness to accept a complete "dépaysement" from everything (and it is understood that one can go as far as to "dépayser" a hand in isolating it from an arm, that this hand profits as a hand, and also that in speaking of "dépayse-ment," we are not only thinking of the possibility of acting in space. ("Avis au lecteur pour 'La Femme 100 Têtes' de Max Ernst," p. 82)

"Let others cling to their family, to their country, and to the earth . . ." (p. 33): the Surrealist takes pride in an isolation from others with their herdlike values, and in his own championship of a permanent "dizzying exchange." The pride itself will in most cases save him from complete breakdown[2]—"and I have never conceived any uncertainty about my own interior equilibrium" (p. 33). Such an inconsistency (see p. 30) should not surprise us.

Balancing the will to multiplicity and complexity is an equally strong will to unity; the latter has, needless to say, nothing whatsoever to do with the traditional notion of simplicity, since it continues to imply and include the multiple. In "Légitime défense," which begins with a eulogy of revolt as the agent of creativity, Breton describes at length the Surrealist's assurance of having been chosen (or "condemned") to answer the call of the marvelous:

It is an order which we have received once and for all and which we have never had an opportunity to dispute. It sometimes seems to us, and it is even rather paradoxical, that what we say is not what is most necessary to say and that there might be a better way of saying it. But it is as if we had been condemned to it for eternity. (p. 56)

The Surrealist writes from a metaphysical and moral need as compelling as any of the usual values accepted by non-Surrealists; and the act of writing effects a major unification of his personality against the exterior social ramifications of ordinary living. The mental state proper to receiving *"le message automatique"* is closely akin to the mental state of the primitive and the child, both of whom demonstrate a unique faculty, dissociated in the adult into the acts of perception and representation (p. 250). The main role of automatism is to re-create the original identification of these two acts within the setting of a monistic ("monotone") esthetics and metaphysics like that propagated by Count Keyserling: "It speaks only of a unique being, where God, the Soul, and the world are united, of the one which is the deepest essence of all multiplicity" (p. 59).

The vision from the state of Surrealist grace is always described as crystalline. Man and the universe are seen to be free from the diverse shadows of traditional categorizations, both individual and social, and of Western rationalism. At the end of his essay on Max Ernst, Breton invokes the "Orient of anger and of pearls" in an intense lyricism based stylistically on the play of dualities typical of Surrealism at its emotional peaks:

You who are the shining image of my dispossession, Orient, beautiful bird of prey and of innocence, I implore you from the depth of the kingdom of shadows! Inspire me, so that I may be he who has no more shadow. (p. 35)

It is natural that the greatest lucidity and illumination should be visible in the works of artists, as they most frequently re-create the unique union of seeing and representing. The essay "Picasso dans son élément" describes the lucid vision of the man freed from all ties, rational, personal, and social, by his "desire for total consciousness . . . the sum of all these needs, of all these experiences of disintegration which will be fulfilled with an *implacable lucidity*" (p. 196). For this man, the world appears to be once more in a state of genesis which Breton calls "the great illumination," the crystalline chain "from which not one link is missing." In the paintings of Picasso runs the "marvelous, irresistible current" of luminous revelation in its harmony and force; in certain "sparkling" moments, the action of the "radiant river" is clearly seen.

It is also over this same "brilliant, inapproachable, magnetized river" that Dali, like Picasso, refuses to lay down any bridges to reassure the average spectator. Here an unusual courage is required for all the Surrealists and participators in the Surrealist vision; they cannot retreat before anything which can in any way enlarge the field of imagination, and they must work for the reconstruction of Noah's ark so that this time "it will not be the dove that comes back, but the crow." Fear threatens them at every step, in all the deserted landscapes of de Chirico, in all the odd re-creations of the artist's haunted fancy. Breton is convinced that unknown beings are lurking: "in a sort of interior window, and they reverberate in *the air* as if the air were suddenly revealed to be a simple trick of glass panes which could be imperceptibly, but definitely, played with so that an immense hole could be made, where there would finally appear the beings—which we may or may not be able to exorcize—haunting a second landscape that we cannot help but suspect" (p. 88). Even these malicious "beings of prey" are to be sought out, since they are so far unknown. Just as the world of erotic imagination is valuable for its "kernel of night," so far not completely explored, so any act or sensation not yet experienced is to be tried. Automatic writing was, Breton confesses in "Le Message automatique" of 1933, valuable above all for its power to clear out the literary stable, to open the floodgates so that the old dull world of the already tried could be swept away.

II *Desire and Motion*

The ideal atmosphere as Breton had said ten years before (in the "Introduction au Discours sur le peu de réalité") is one in which "what could exist destroys at every step what does exist." Nothing is inadmissible, there is no wish which cannot be carried out, even that of the frog who would like to be bigger than the ox. La Fontaine called such an animal foolish—not so the Surrealist: "It did not seem to me that any wish, even an animal one and of such a puerile kind, was incapable of perfect execution" (p. 32). The whole point of artistic creation is to "affirm the hostility" which the creative being feels toward the exterior world and to "render the exterior object adequate to his desire, and thus to reconcile, to a certain extent, the being and the world . . ." ("Picasso dans son élément," p. 197). It is unquestionably valuable to express the "dialectical movement" of the mind. The finished work, however, is to be considered only an excretion in relation to the primary desire:

Since it alone is truly suggestive of the power granted to man to act on the world to make it conform to himself (and in this way it is a fully revolutionary power), the uninterrupted temptation to confront all that exists with all that can exist, to bring forth from the never seen everything that can exhort the already seen to make itself less obvious seems far more precious to me. (p. 198)

Picasso's paintings convert the entire world to their own transparency, permit it to be reborn in an "interminable gestation" of *optimal* moments, for against the illusory power of the external world the human will forms other beings as instants of intercession. Picasso never loses sight of the ephemeral nature of his creations, and it is in them that his work finds its particular *temporary* radiance.

The character of the Surrealist creation is constant motion; no Surrealist work proposes itself as eternal. If Breton envisages himself as a Theseus forever closed within a labyrinth of crystal, at least he intends to confer upon the labyrinth a movement as perpetual as his within it. Speaking of the poetry of René Char (in his "Lettre à A. Rolland de Renéville"), Breton praises his crystalline union of transparency and hardness and takes for his definition of crystallization the Hegelian description of "the moment when the mobile and unresting activity of magnetism attains complete repose." He will echo, in other terms, this paradoxical union of movement and rest in his later definition of convulsive beauty, the beauty he thinks most appropriate to Surrealism. But here he means to stress, rather than beauty, the inescapable and dynamic Hegelian dialectic of the mind:

For my part I hold resolutely to this conception of thought which never ceases to oscillate between the consciousness of its perfect autonomy and that of its strict dependency. . . . As a consequence, I count, for the future liberation of human thought, at once on the sovereignty never yet realized within this thought alone and still always potentially contained there, and on the future of the exterior facts which is always susceptible to influence. (p. 131)

Breton's optimism is based on man's ability to change his own language and thought processes and with them, the world. The unknown is seen as a constant inspiration to action and to the mobility in which Breton places his ultimate faith.

CHAPTER 6

La Cle des champs (1936-52)

In spite of the number, the chronological range, and the apparently diverse subjects of these essays, the central theme here is more closely defined than in earlier collections. One would not say, of course, that they were written in strict adherence to an *a priori* topic, but that at this point the forcefulness of the Surrealist attitude is such as to convey not just an intensity of feeling, but an actual coherence of theme and structure. Taken together, the essays of this collection comprise a convincing statement on the Surrealist revolution—on its rejection of the world as given, on the means it advocates for enlarging and conveying the Surrealist poetic vision (the adjectives being treated as strict equivalents by Breton), and on its aim of re-creating the world and simultaneously, the human understanding.

I *Disorientation*

"Devant le rideau," Breton's commentary on the Surrealist exhibition of 1947, is an impassioned defense of the group's attitude, which he defines as "the *great disorientation,* no longer in a limited space like a game of blindman's buff, but in all space and in all time, without keeping the least point of reference" (p. 90). This is, he says, the same attitude that the Surrealists had recommended in front of the blank page: a total throwing-off of any past—of memory, of knowledge, of proven talent—for a total future liberty of inspiration granted *spontaneously.* He adopts for a motto a formula created by the Roumanian Surrealists—*"La connaissance par la méconnaissance"* (knowledge through miscomprehension) —and calls for the "categorical refusal of the conditions of life and thought inflicted on man in the middle of the twentieth century" (p. 91), a refusal which implies a certain ascetic strength, as he freely admits. In a footnote to this passage he emphasizes

the point that this attitude is the exact opposite of that adopted by
some former members of the Belgian Surrealist group, gathered
around the painter René Magritte, who made a decision to let into
their works only "charm, pleasure, sun, desirable objects" to the
exclusion of anything that signified "sadness, anguish, threatening
objects." Even if this was a desperate measure on their part to conform to the resolution of a political group to whose orders they
were committed, it would be hard not to compare such a decision
to that of a child who might decide to immobilize the needle of
the barometer at "fair" to keep the weather good. Already ten
years earlier, the famous essay "Le Merveilleux contre le mystère"
(which opens *La Clé des champs*) begins with the same "refusal
of life as it is given to us."

Nonacceptance is the starting point of Surrealism, as of Dada;
whether it is considered a purely negative phenomenon or the
initial impulse for a positive program, this point cannot be over-
looked at any stage. Built into any theory acceptable to Surrealism, it guarantees that enough flexibility be maintained for a
constant questioning. One of the most moving and most revealing
statements Breton ever made was that when the attitudes of
Surrealism had themselves become unacceptable, he would be the
first to align himself with the successor to Surrealism. It is less
important to debate whether in fact Surrealism did or will become
"out of date" than to recognize the genuine feeling behind his
statement.

In "Le Mécanicien," an essay on the stories of Jean Ferry,
Breton honors all the works "electrified by this need of subversion"[1] that the individual is obliged to demonstrate against the
evidence of a general "domestication." If, however, the means used
to subvert are poor, the attempt will be gravely compromised. The
scandal presented by the world grows from day to day and the
Surrealist must bear witness to it in a properly Surrealist fashion.
(That is, he must be careful not simply to borrow methods from
other "movements" whose range and potentiality will not suffice
for the peculiar intensity of the Surrealist revolution.) The
primary weapon of subversion recommended in "Le Mécanicien"
is that of the dream, which will both undermine the pinnings of the
"active" world and redeem it. Breton seconds Ferry's invitation to
"cultivate the dream, to make it produce all it can by any means

whatsoever and especially by the most 'difficult' means" (p. 221).
Surrealism is never to be "easy," rather the exact opposite; the
Surrealists take a perfectly justified pride in the difficulty, the
obscurity of their theories and their creations, both for its own
sake and as a defiance of what they judge to be the superficial,
nonrevolutionary facility of the non-Surrealist posture.

The title essay of the collection attacks Christianity, rationalism,
and art criticism as the three elements which have been responsible
for the sheeplike and ineffably dull character of the public mind.
But the tone, even of the title, is completely positive: "L'Art des
fous, la clé des champs." Being without rational constraint or
purpose, the insane man (*"le fou"*) is in a state of liberty never
felt before except in the primitives, who also have their own
structures thought of by Breton as less oppressive than ours. The
art of the "insane"[2] cannot be appreciated within the narrow
boundaries in which logic usually confines us; so we, the public,
must enjoy the art before trying to "understand" it, and the critics
should do the same. Contemplation of such art has the salutary
effect of planting in our minds the seeds of *doubt,* "this healthy
doubt which will open the path of a superior and serene intelligence" (p. 221).

II   *The Marvelous and the Open*

All the essays of this collection, insisting as they do on what is
termed in the first one "a rejection of the real world which can
only end with this world," urge a simultaneous "law of pure and
simple abandonment to the *marvelous,* in this abandonment resid-
ing the only source of eternal communication between men" ("Le
Merveilleux contre le mystère," pp. 8, 12). The marvelous is not
to be confused with the mysterious, which is *sought* and is therefore the sign of a weakness and a lack. The latter can be the
product of work and effort, while the former is a matter of passion,
like love. One succumbs to it rather than choosing it; it is of
necessity spontaneous rather than calculated. The link between
this notion of the marvelous and the value set on dreams, on revelations of chance and of automatic procedures, and on the mind
of the mentally abnormal is clear. In all these cases, the "seer" or
listener[3] renounces the "critical intelligence of his acts. Lucidity is
the great enemy of revelation" (p. 10). In such a context,

Breton's hesitation to cut open some Mexican jumping beans (in the company of the psychoanalyst Lacan and others) to see what was really inside is particularly interesting.

For him, as he explains in "Fronton-Virage," knowledge instantly impairs the sense of wonder and *stops* the possibility of deliberation within the human mind. Therefore, it is, in "marvelous" situations, to be avoided as long as possible. Breton contradicts the version recounted by Caillois and Etiemble, both of whom claimed he refused ever to open the beans. His philosophy is not *"obscurantiste,"* he says:

> I insist on this nuance characteristic of my way of thinking . . . that they would not be opened until we had exhausted the discussion about the *probable* cause of the movements. . . . I was in no way opposed to this investigation and if I wanted to delay it a bit, I still considered it necessary. It is obvious that the idea I held and continue to hold of magic would have kept me from wanting to "save" it so cheaply. We were after all adults: I restricted myself to the demand that the mind be used more seriously before calling on the flat testimony of the eyes. (p. 186)[4]

In the place of a *closed rationalism* and a *closed realism,* which are unitary concepts, Breton recommends the *open rationalism* and *open realism* described by the philosopher Gaston Bachelard.[5] The means of opening our theories and our minds are identical with those he calls the "key to the fields," the fictional and the imaginary. Fiction, the counterforce to the world of the real, is the realm in which we must locate a new collective myth appropriate for our epoch as the Gothic novel was for the nineteenth century. All the "electric" currents it carried (miraculous apparitions, and what Breton calls the *light* of overwhelming coincidence) are more alive than ever and are waiting to be embodied in the new form we must elaborate. A collective sensitivity (*"prise de conscience commune de la vie"*) is necessary for the general liberation of the modern mind (*"Limites non—frontières du surrealisme"*).

In the essay "Comme dans un bois," Breton quotes Malcolm de Chazal's theory of the night as a key (*"clé d'ouverture"*) in that it is able to vanquish all the logical antinomies; these antinomies haunt Surrealism, which seeks to overcome them and still to preserve the tension which they create. Breton had given a lyrical

description of them in the first essay of the collection, explaining
that since they had existed prior to our social system, they are
likely not to disappear even when it does:

These antinomies should be overcome because they are felt as cruel, in
that they also imply a slavery, but one more definitive and deeper than
temporal slavery, and this suffering, like the other, must not find man
resigned to it. These antinomies are those of waking and sleeping
(reality and the dream), reason and madness, the objective and the
subjective, perception and representation, the past and the future, the
collective sense and love, and of life and death themselves. (p. 18)

For Breton, as he explains in "Comme dans un bois," the cinema
is the most obvious and general fiction possible, the "only absolutely modern mystery." ("Mystery" has here the medieval sense
of general public celebration as well as its more usual sense;
Breton mentions explicitly that one goes to the cinema as one
might to a church.) A film brings about a total *dépaysement* from
the real, daytime world, and yet links that world to the world of
night (or the imagination). It is itself a highly developed *"clé
d'ouverture"* as it encourages the mechanism of correspondences
on which all Surrealist realizations depend for their range and their
depth.

A more primitive form of mystery is the "halo" seen by the
Surrealists around certain objects created by less "civilized"
peoples. These objects stimulate the poetic (Surrealist) view of
things, characterized by its triumph over the dualities of perception and representation, of the physical and the mental. Incarna-
tions of the "poetic sublime," they offer us brief and startling
glances toward *"autre chose"* that we cannot know by our intelligence alone ("Océanie").

Poetry and art are both to some extent refutations of the book
and the theater. "I am not afraid to say that Surrealism attacked
the sense of the book itself . . ." (p. 64). Breton is now convinced,
even though he had collaborated in the writing as well as in the
presentation of early Surrealist (and Dada) plays, that the theater,
like literature, is often slow to act on the modern imagination, that
it is less easily electrified with subversive tendencies. For him,
writings of Valéry and of Proust are invalidated by their nonrele-

vance to the moment; Apollinaire, in spite of his enormous gifts
and sense of intellectual adventure and his realization that it was
still necessary to *"toucher à l'essence du Verbe"* (disturb the very
nature of the Word) was betrayed by his determination to cele-
brate France's participation in World War I (relevant, perhaps,
but mistaken in Breton's view).

Breton propounds the above ideas in his speech to the French
students at Yale in 1942 (called "Situation du surréalisme entre
les deux guerres"), where he rejoices at the demise of so-called
rationality and tells them of the Surrealist faith in the *"genius* of
youth." He makes at the same time a detailed résumé of Surrealist theory in its advocacy of dialectical processes (those of
Heraclituś, of Meister Eckhart, and of Hegel: Surrealism is, as
the reader will have already noticed, as eclectic as it is impassioned), of a community of spirit like that of the Middle Ages, of
its revision of methods of knowledge to include the revelation of
the unconscious (automatism, and the associated reliance on
chance events as "manifestations of exterior necessity clearing a
path in the human unconscious," so reconciling man and the
world external to him) and finally, of the humor it calls black
which serves as an escape valve for the disillusion provoked by the
world insofar as it is still unrevolutionized. Above all, says Breton,
Surrealism has succeeded, even while expressing the anguish of its
time, in giving a "new configuration to *beauty*" (p. 73).

III   *Analogy and Necessity*

Two essays of 1947 serve as the basis for a Surrealist criterion
of style and of judgment: "Signe ascendant" is an extensive
elaboration of the Surrealist conviction that nothing is gratuitous,
that everything demonstrates a certain necessity which could always
be deciphered if only we knew the code. Not only are things exterior to us linked to each other, but we are linked to them in ways
which our conscious mind is unable to comprehend. What the
experiences of objective chance (*"le hasard objectif,"* a general
term which includes the specific discoveries of found objects and
expressions called *"objets trouvés"* and *"trouvailles"*) and automatic writing, speaking, and drawing, show is the more personal
correspondences between our predictions and our future, our

hidden desires and their unexpected fulfillment which we might
not otherwise have recognized. Any method is valuable if it leads
to the production of analogies, which Breton describes as the

spontaneous, extra-lucid, insolent relationship which is established,
under certain conditions, between one thing and another that common
sense would never think of bringing together. (p. 111)

The primordial contacts have been cut: these contacts, I say, that only
the analogical impulse succeeds fleetingly in reestablishing. Whence the
importance assumed, at distant intervals, by these brief and infrequent
sparklings of the lost mirror. (p. 113)

To bring two things together into a previously untried juxtaposition
is the surest way of developing new vision, a new language, and
thus, a new universe which would never have been visible within
the *sequential* framework of ordinary logical perception and expression (A,B,C,D,E . . .). The Surrealist places A with E, never
concerning himself with what should precede or follow what; all
elements are seen as simultaneous.

"Comète surréaliste" lists as the first article of the Surrealist
program: "to maintain plastic expression in a state of incessant
potential recreation in order to translate human desire in its constant fluctuation." It is not only flexibility and energy of style
which matter, it is also the community of experience and expression. To be sure, the forms of collective desire are scattered as well
as highly individualized, but they can be made to converge at
the point of a new myth, the existence of which serves to confirm
the "indivisible Surrealist pact between men," in Breton's phrase.
He once again mentions the beings or objects *"à halo,"* with the
aura of the sacred about them, and demands a specific *initiation* by
poetry or art to the universe toward which they gesture.

And it is here that the initial step in the Surrealist program—
"the great disorientation"—leads clearly to its end, in the sense of
its purpose. Against the traditional pose of both painters and street
merchants, with their hands on their hips like men in the form of
jugs (a fatalistic pose signifying the keeping of the status quo while
waiting for a better world), Breton shouts: "Enough jug-men."

Surrealism's absolute rejection of both the *realistic* and the *abstract* is of a moral order rather than an esthetic one:

Non-Surrealist and, to our way of thinking, regressive, is any work turned toward the daily spectacle of beings and things, that is, participating immediately in the animal, vegetable, and mineral furniture which surrounds us even if the latter should be rendered optically unrecognizable by being "deformed." The Surrealist work banishes resolutely anything in the realm of *simple* perception, whatever intellectual speculation is grafted on it to modify appearances. If the jug remains enemy number one here, it is understood that the Surrealist means to put in the same sack the little ship, the bouquet of anemones, and the obliging lady who used to pose either dressed or naked. (p. 100)

Abstract art, on the other hand, represents an abdication of human desire and a rupture with the precious human perception and thought which Surrealism would like to reconcile. The criterion of Surrealist art is not, as is often thought, any particular technique, but rather the spirit in which it was conceived [6]—it is for this reason that Surrealism can be seen as a movement of genuinely moral intent. The end of each of Breton's essays is strong, from that point of view especially. In this one, he gives a summary, brief and poetic, of the triple goal which it is the *honor* of the Surrealist poets and artists to fulfill insofar as possible: "to bring about a social liberation, to work unceasingly for the complete removal of the accumulated encrustations imprisoning our customs, and to reconstruct dramatically the human understanding" (p. 105).

The recurrent appeal of all these essays is to passion and to the spirit of youth as its ideal embodiment. The old rationalistic world has again and again proved the emptiness of its values, which have led only to war and to unhappiness. Revolt is inseparable from generosity, individual creation and understanding from collective feeling in the over-all task of promoting a "libertarian" world ("some say a Surrealist world, but it is the same"—"La Claire tour," p. 273). The best description of the re-created world is that promised by the alchemist ("Behold, I shall renew all things"— "Fronton-Virage"), a world into which one is finally initiated in an extreme step that "leads the self beyond any conditioned state whatsoever." [7] That the Surrealists think such a transcendence of our ordinary human conditions possible is perhaps a proof of their irrationality. But since it is precisely on that *dépassement* of "normality," of normal conditions, and of reason that their revolution is based, the criticism is not seen by them as negative, rather as a positive testimony to the unity of their motives and their way of expressing them. Their words are addressed to the young, who will understand them, and to the passionate, who will agree with them.

CHAPTER 7

Le Surréalisme et la peinture

Breton's essays on art share with all his work a style of passionate conviction and a lyricism rarely surpassed in the
French language. Their interest depends little on one's acquaintance with the particular artists about whom Breton is writing—at
the risk of sounding heretical, one might say in fact that many of
the descriptions are interchangeable from artist to artist. That this
should be so even to a minor degree is a witness to the strength of
Breton's own personality, since there is certainly no lack of individuality on the part of the artists.

I *Expectation*

Plastic art is, like fiction, an ideal setting for the "great disorientation" on which Surrealism depends, or the sense of a *"trouble
moderne"* which it incarnates. At its best it can have the same
socially *isolating* effect as the works of Lautréamont, Rimbaud,
Mallarmé, separating the human mind from traditional back-
grounds: "the words family, country, society, seem to us macabre
jokes" (p. 15). Nor is the separation a merely social one. Breton
recounts the power certain canvases have always held over him;
he feels himself lost in the space between their frames, their
reality overcoming not only the reality of the world beyond them
but also his own personal identity. "I lost, without being able to
help myself, the sense of my role" (p. 13). Another statement
which has all the ambiguity of the most celebrated Surrealist
aphorisms might be assimilated to the preceding one: "For *we are
not,* in literature and in art" (p. 39). The life of the canvas or the
page takes over from our life so that we are only what it is. The
Surrealist lives in a permanent expectation of experiences, sensations. He is not willing to treat anything as a simple object, confined to a single purpose and placed in the world for just that

57

purpose. At any point, a revelation could come from the least expected source. "Nothing that surrounds us is an object for us, for us everything is a subject" (p. 59).

And on the other hand, it is up to us to make of the non-fictional world a work of art. Everything is affected by our gaze upon it, and for the Surrealists it is a matter of ultimate importance to realize that one's interior desire controls one's vision. Hamlet's clouds were not *like* animals, they *were* animals, since he saw them as such. "There are no landscapes. Not even a horizon" (p. 68). Our own thoughts surround the physical, dominating it completely. If this seems to contradict certain of the above statements, such uncomfortable ambiguity is characteristic of Surrealism. We are masters, by our imagination, of the exterior universe. We are by the same token subject to our own imagining of it, and to that of the artists whose vision we cannot help but share, in a sort of double servitude which is also a double mastery of reality:

Figures of our suspicion, beautiful sad shadows who surround our cavern, we know that you are shadows. The *great subjective light* inundating the canvases of Tanguy is the one which leaves us the least alone, in the least deserted place. No creature here who does not participate metaphorically in the life we choose to live, who does not answer the expectation which is ours. . . (p. 69).

Breton finally insists that in Tanguy's paintings we can see very clearly the mental world which is just beginning ("qui en est à la Genèse").

For Breton, paintings must above all not reinforce what is already seen and would exist without them, for that would be making a pitiful use of the "magic power" of the artist's hand, a use which Breton condemns in his strongest terms as "an inexcusable abdication." Any work of art must refer to a *"purely interior model* or it will not exist." [1] Based on the imagination, it must create reality, not preserve it in its usual form. The painter deliberately practices the crime of *"lèse-réalité,"* refusing to permit objects their ordinary associations. When Breton praises Jean Arp, it is for his daring to rearrange the most everyday elements, so that they seem to acquire totally new necessities and uses, as do the newly arranged words of the Surrealist language:

With Arp, the hour of distribution has gone by. The word "table" was a begging word: to write. . . . In reality, if it is now understood what we mean by that, a nose is perfectly at home beside a chair, it even takes on the form of a chair. . . . The birds have never sung better than in this aquarium. (p. 71)

Breton repeatedly emphasizes the courage which is required for undertaking his mental adventure. Only the "fever of *total conquest*" could inspire travelers to set out on "the mysterious road where fear awaits us at every step, where the desire we have to turn back is overcome only by the fallacious hope of being accompanied" (p. 16). Certain artists, like Picasso, paint canvases so illuminated that they cast light over the whole path the others must travel; others, like de Chirico, show a purely interior illumination—but all true Surrealist paintings point the way to a "future continent" and manifest a genuine faith that "each person is able to accompany an Alice always more beautiful to a wonderland" (p. 19). Breton calls the Surrealist adventure an *"engagement héroïque,"* a heroic commitment to leaving the prey for the shadow, all that is certain and visible for what is uncertain and so far nonexistent except within the realm of the imagination.

II *Commitment and Connection*

But, as we have already seen, it is not permitted to the Surrealist simply to turn his back on reality. The temptation to idealism is only temporary: Surrealism goes beyond it toward a dialectical reality, a dramatic and constant interchange between the real and the sur-real or super-real:

Everything I love, all I think and feel, inclines me toward a particular philosophy of immanence according to which surreality is contained in reality itself and is neither superior nor exterior to it. And reciprocally, for the container is also the contained. It is almost a matter of a communicating vessel between the containing and the contained. (p. 69)

And it is only by including the real with the unreal that Surrealist paintings can possibly meet the final challenge, posed not by a rival kind of art but by the *genuine* anguish of the "real" world.

Wonderlands can be esthetically perfect and still crumble at the test of human suffering. Breton demands that paintings hold good not only when compared with real wheat fields but with famine, which is far more difficult. Surrealists must somehow manage to retain their "haughty feelings of discontinuity" (a notion closely related to their voluntary disorientation), their aloofness from the human situation and from the judgment of others ("we are better than what we *pass for,*" p. 70), and yet not lose contact with the non-Surrealist world. As time goes on, the disorientation and the aloofness submit more and more to the involvement and moral commitment, but the latter has been unmistakably present to some extent from the beginning.

The "primitivism" of the Surrealist group serves them as a criterion for utterly scorning works of art based on historical and civilized visions of the world; however, it offers no excuse for trivial or uncommitted art. Max Ernst, for instance, puts into question not the surface arrangement but "the substance of objects, gives it complete licence to decide once more on the shadow, the pose and the form of the objects" (pp. 53–54). Ernst serves as a good example of the difficulty Breton deems an essential part of the heroic commitment to challenge our ordinary perception of things, "in order to break completely with them, more especially with the ease their accustomed aspect shows to us . . ." (p. 170). Ernst undertakes the gigantic task of an entire re-creation, bringing with him the pieces of the labyrinth which cannot be fitted back together the way they once were: "It was like creation's game of solitaire: all the pieces, unbelievably separated from each other, no longer aware of any particular magnetism one for another, tried to find new affinities" (p. 50). This time everything is reconstituted in *favor of the image,* as in poetry. But beyond the superhuman effort on our part there is an intense resistance on the part of these now disparate elements which adopt attitudes of unrelenting hostility toward each other. To be a mediator, like Ernst, is to be a gambler: "To play all for all. In that resides perhaps the possibility of living for Max Ernst, of living freely, perhaps it is in that that his deep humanity consists" (p. 50).

"Lyricism, characteristic of all the works we admire": this quality is not to be confused with the traditionally "lyric" style, since it refers not to style, but to vision, and since it is far removed from tradition in all senses. This sort of poetic vision is best exemplified by Breton's statement that when the artist brings together elements at random, the minor possibility that any of these elements might have met before is *"lyrique par excellence"* (p. 51). As for the style of Surrealism, it is, as one might suppose, the dramatic counterpoise of an everyday monotonous style suited only to the "flat testimony of our eyes." Surrealist vision is like that of an intelligent and extraordinarily gifted child, and the Surrealist style must not betray that vision by a dull "realism": "it is permitted to ask of the real nothing but the superexpressive, the expressive in the most childish sense, and not to go beyond this expressive."

Surrealist art does not have to do what nonSurrealist art does; it has never to perfectly represent what we see or feel. It has only to lay down a series of connecting wires (*"fils conducteurs"*) between things not joined before, to make over the world in the image of our interior conception, to make it fit our dream. It does not necessarily follow that we will be enticed into every Surrealist canvas we see; the world re-created by certain Surrealists young or old may possibly not fit our vision, or not communicate its own to us. Breton always leaves room for our individual judgment: "Seeing, hearing, is nothing. Recognizing or not recognizing is everything. Between what I recognize and what I do not recognize there is myself. And what I do not recognize, I shall continue not to recognize" (p. 66).

CHAPTER 8

Love, Madness, and Solitude

I   Nadja

Je préfère encore une fois, marcher dans la nuit à me croire celui qui marche dans le jour. (Again, I prefer walking in the night to believing myself to be walking in the daylight, *Nadja*, p. 55.)

In *Le Surréalisme et la peinture* Breton represents the painter André Derain (who was original enough to concern himself, for instance, not with the weight of the glass of water upon the table, but with the pressure of the table upward on the glass) as reproducing a definite *"trouble moderne."* The opening line of *Nadja*, "Who am I?" can be taken just as easily for an example of the disturbed mind, since it leads directly to another question: "Whom do I haunt?", the latter word revealing between the author and certain other beings "relationships more singular, less avoidable, more troubling than I would have thought."

In spite of the title, the initial and indeed the principal subject of the book is not Nadja's search for self-identity but Breton's. Nadja, whose name is the beginning of the Russian word for hope (and only the beginning) does not enter the book until after the first third of the text, and she fades out of it in the last part. She is important only as a stage in Breton's autobiography, as an example of the possible genius of the mentally abnormal and of their inexcusable treatment in "asylums," and as a contrast with the more "adaptable" behavior of the author and his friends. She troubles his mind temporarily, but she can in no way affect his general comportment or his permanent sentiments. This is a pitifully one-sided love story, for Nadja, who loves Breton as "the sun," is finally found by him to be less interesting then the more "normal" woman to whom the end of the book is addressed.

Breton undertakes the book then, not as a testimonial to the extraordinary character whose title it bears, but as an inquiry into what is individual about himself. What part of his personality continues through all the events which he experiences, all the gestures he makes, in the unique tastes he recognizes himself as having, and how does this individuality separate him from others? (It is scarcely necessary to point out that Nadja's separation from the mass of human beings is in some less drastic way paralleled by Breton's.) As if one had asked the question: "Why should one go to any length to discover one's own difference?", Breton answers:

Isn't it true that in the extent to which I become conscious of this differentiation I shall find out what I came to do in this world among all the other people and of what unique message I am the bearer, answering for it with my life? (p. 9)

But he refuses to consider this exploration of his life a return upon his footsteps (like the image of a ghost conjured up by the expression "haunt") because the footsteps are in no way lost. (Nor are those of the first book of essays unambiguously lost, since *Les Pas perdus* might be read as meaning "The Not Lost" as well as "The Lost Steps.") All the ideas connected with Christianity like loss, the fall, penance, are totally opposed by the Surrealist way of thought, which confers upon the same terms a contrary sense.

So is the idea of an author's deliberate mystification: it is essential to know the way in which any man looks at certain things. An author has no right to hide the key to his books, to surround his characters with superficial mystery, changing the color of the heroine's hair from blonde to brunette so as to protect the real woman behind the story. For Breton, the only interesting works are left ajar like doors and can be entered by anyone:

As for me, I shall continue to inhabit my glass house, where anyone coming to visit me can be seen at any hour . . . where I rest at night on a glass bed with glass sheets, where *what I am* will appear to me sooner or later traced with a diamond. (pp. 17–18)[1]

Events will not be covered over with a polite façade—for his own attitude toward Nadja, which may seem heartless to the reader, he will make no excuses.

The entry for the eleventh of October betrays a complete lack of
sensitivity: "What is more, Nadja arrived late and I do not expect
from her anything exceptional. We wander along the streets, near
each other, but very separate. . . . It is aggravating to see her
reading the menus on restaurant doors and juggling the names of
certain dishes. I am bored" (pp. 103–4). Whether such intensity
is here, or is always, compensated for by an equal sincerity is not
the sort of judgment a Surrealist or his reader is asked to make,
falling as it does within the realm of standard ethical questions and
therefore outside the Surrealist realm, which is nothing if not
nonstandard.

Secondly, the lack of order in this "novel" is planned. Breton
will in all cases prefer chance to orderly calculation, the "caprice
of the moment" to a preconceived system. His purpose is to relate
only

The most significant episodes of my life *such as I conceive it outside
of its organic design,* that is in the extent to which it is subjugated to
chance happenings, to the smallest as to the greatest, where protesting
against the usual idea I have of it, it introduces me into a sort of
forbidden world of sudden relationships, petrifying coincidences, of
reflexes taking the lead over any mental reaction, of chords struck as
on the piano, of sparks that one could see by, but really *see,* if they
were not even more rapid than the others. (pp. 18–19)

Certain facts or observations take on the appearance of *signals,*
even when one is not sure what they are designating; rather than
confuse them with the mass of ordinary facts, Breton simply sup-
presses the latter—hence the odd atmosphere of the work. Even
among the significant facts, there is as great a range as between
totally "automatic" texts which come freely, and the "reflective"
ones, for which the author bears the responsibility. (It is obvious
that Breton is not averse to arrangements, distinctions, and to
"ordering" as such, only insofar as they represent a logic he finds
imprisoning.) He says of the signal-facts:

These facts could be ranked in a hierarchy from the simplest to the
most complex, from the special, indefinable movement provoked by
the sight of some unusual objects[2] or by our arrival in such and such
a place, accompanied by the very clear sensation that for us something

serious, something essential is involved, to the complete inability to be at peace with ourselves produced by certain trains of events, certain groups of circumstances which go far beyond our understanding, and, in most cases, permit no return to a rational activity unless we call on our instinct of conservation. A great quantity of intermediate steps could be set up between those "faits-glissades" and these "faits-précipices." (p. 20)

The images from which the last two terms are derived indicate Breton's attitude toward "real" experiences: they are most valuable to him when they lead away from themselves to a set of "irrational" feelings and actions, and the more directly they lead there, the more valuable they are. The *"précipice"* or cliff over which one is bound to fall unless preserved by the life instinct is to be infinitely preferred to the *"glissade"* or slope which one could, if overtaken by panic, reascend by means of one's own resources of intelligence. Surrealism places a higher value on risk than on safety, on intensity than on reasonableness or intellect. The facts of which one is only the "haggard witness" take precedence over those whose details and outcomes are easily discerned, so that by implication it is better to be forced to look than to see voluntarily. The structure of *Nadja,* insofar as it needs or finds justification, functions only as a support for these facts, and has no more cohesion than they do. Possibly *Nadja* itself could function as a *"fait-glissade"* for the reader (if not as a *"fait-précipice"*) since created works serve as experiences, and since in fact Breton does say he writes in the effort to provoke the same sorts of sensations he has experienced. An honest recognition of the ability to find pride and even pleasure in the danger implied by the images of sliding and falling, although it is not by any means confined to Surrealist psychology, is essential to the understanding of all Surrealist work.

In all these respects, *Nadja* serves as an indispensable introduction to the theory of Surrealism. There are, of course, variations as the movement develops, the most obvious being, perhaps, the attitude toward automatic writing and the degree of the author's responsibility: Breton will eventually regret that so much importance was attached to it, claiming that in fact the mind was always to some extent the director of the hand. But when, in 1963, he re-edits *Nadja,* the changes are not major ones. He insists, in the introduction to the new edition, on its "antiliterary" quality, the abundant photographic illustration having for its object the elimination of all descriptions (attacked in the first manifesto) and the tone of medical observation undermining the notion of literary style for the benefit of a spontaneous document. Breton believes the purposely bare style of *Nadja,* its *"dénument volontaire,"* to be largely responsible for its wide audience, since this very nonornamentation enables its vanishing point (*"point de fuite"*) to recede far beyond the ordinary limits of vision. Like the images of *glissade* and the *précipice,* that of *fuite* indicates motion from one level or location to another. Motion is a constant of Surrealist thought and theory, and Nadja, the wandering soul, is perhaps the perfect Surrealist.

By describing, in no particular order, a series of these unusual objects and the unusual sensations or realizations which *necessarily* accompany them— a copy of Rimbaud with other poems inserted, one blue glove of a surprising weight, as if it were pressing on another hand, and the optical illusion of a sign reading "Maison Rouge" which seems from another angle to read "Police," representing by coincidence the repressive authorities and connected by irrational but "inevitable" circumstances to the illusion of a picture representing a tiger or a vase or an angel depending on the angle of vision—Breton intends to reveal the impossibility or "at least the grave insufficiency" of any so-called rigorous calculation about the notion of personality and the motives for our actions. This, he hopes, will send a number of people into the streets, the street being the obvious place for chance encounters, where mystery can easily prevail over calculations of all sorts, and where sudden attractions,[3] ambiguous situations, and reversals of attitude abound. Nadja herself is the "always inspired and inspiring creature who only liked to be in the street, for her the only place of valid experience, in the street in reach of the questions of any human being who has thrown himself into a great chimerical question" (p. 113).

Breton places a great value on any situation which potentially disturbs his mental habits. The ideal one he gives as an example, that is, of meeting a beautiful naked woman in the forest, is not only unlikely but no longer meaningful once he has expressed the desire (because it would then leave the realm of the spontaneous for that of the predicted); however, his brief discussion of the example is particularly interesting.

> It seems to me that *everything* would have stopped short, ah! I wouldn't be writing what I am writing. I adore this situation in which more than in any other I would probably have lost my *presence of mind*. I would not have even had enough to flee. (Those who laugh at this last sentence are pigs.) (p. 34)

This would, without question, be a *"fait-précipice,"* and yet Breton uses not an image of falling, but of stopping. If he had the presence of mind to call on his instinct of conservation, he would be able to move, yet he does not. At the height of Surrealist adventure, then, there is a sudden cessation of the motion which has led up to it: at one point of *Les Vases communicants* Breton recommends retreat to the calm center of the tornado. Nadja's entire life, she admits, consists of telling herself stories, and Breton comments that this sort of life is the extreme limit of Surrealist aspiration. Nevertheless, directly after this admission, when Breton asks her where she will go upon leaving him at his door, she remarks how easy it is to begin by going back to the place where they were. It is precisely as if there were no idea of progress at all on the personal level, as if all the references to "one day" and "there will be" referred only to communication or liberation in the social realm.

The famous definition at the end of the book—"Beauty will be CONVULSIVE or will not be"—might lead one to suppose that the Surrealist "esthetic" was based only on movement. But the preceding paragraphs are indispensable to its comprehension. Breton has insisted that beauty is neither completely dynamic nor completely static: "It is like a train that starts up in the Lyon station when I know it is never going to leave, that it has not left. It is made of jolts [*"saccades"*] many of which have scarcely any importance but we know they bring on a final *Jolt* which has enormous importance" (p. 154). This image should be considered in connection with another which is its exact reverse, that is, the speeding train stopped in the forest (an image to be discussed later). Breton wants to indicate in this passage "the exact expiration of this movement" as well as the "relationship linking the object in its movement and in its repose." Like the image of the

communicating vessels of reality and surreality, these last images
are combinations of opposites, whose resolution is never a reduction and never a simplification.

"It is possible that this desperate chase will stop here? Chase
after what, I do not know, but *chase,* to bring into play all the
artifices of mental seduction" (p. 109). Breton has by now traced
all the elements composing his *"lumière propre,"* the particular
lighting in which his nature is best visible. And here he places the
mystery of Nadja's personality, which is in so many other places
considered antipathetic to his, in close conjunction to his own.
Instead of "Who am I?", we now hear the question:

Who were we in front of reality, this reality which I now perceive
curled up at Nadja's feet like a naughty dog? . . . How did it come
about that projected together once and for all so far from the earth,
we were able in the brief intervals which our marvelous stupor ac-
corded us, to exchange a few looks of incredible agreement above the
smoking remains of the old thought and this neverceasing life? (p. 110)

But even if Breton considers reality to be subjected to Nadja's
power, he is totally unable to share for any sustained period of
time in her purely intuitive and detached way of conducting herself in the everyday world where he feels himself forced to live.
She is beyond it and irremediably beyond him, neither listening to
his words nor noticing his *ennui,* and so he feels himself incapable
of helping her resolve her many difficulties "normally." Whether
we are intended to concentrate on the irony latent in the latter
expression is unclear. In any case, the split between Nadja's
feelings and those of Breton is pitifully clear, and it is pathetic
from all sides. As we have seen, Breton always makes a sharp
distinction between what is valuable and what is not, from his
(that is, the Surrealist) viewpoint; Nadja on the other hand, does
not judge between moments, does not separate them according to
their interest:

I had, long since, ceased to get along with Nadja very well. To tell the
truth, perhaps we never agreed, at least on the manner of looking at
the simple things of existence. She had chosen once and for all not
to pay any attention, not to care about the hour, not to make any
distinction between the idle talk she sometimes made and the other kind

that mattered so much to me, not to take any notice of my passing moods and of the more or less serious difficulty I had in pardoning her worst distractions. (p. 125)

While she narrates the details of "the most lamentable" circumstances of her life, Breton is "reduced to waiting, with a frown," for her to move on to something else. (Needless to say, it is not a question of their moving together toward something else.) Breton is accustomed to accepting the passive role in front of the marvelous, but he demands that the marvelous be *constantly* marvelous. Consequently he never expects Nadja to be "natural," or like other women, and it is the fact that she is not perpetually interesting in what he calls her "exercises" (in the mental sense) which cannot be forgiven. In fact, the "exercises" which Eluard and Breton did together of mental aberrations, that is, their imitations of the style of those aberrations, are beautiful, and they are interesting. *L'Immaculée conception* (the title they give to these exercises) is never as dull as Nadja seems to Breton; but then it is the work of two poets.

Nadja, Breton says, does not have a "real conception of her value. . . . ." If he had only loved her, in the sense he means love ("mysterious, improbable, unique, confusing and indubitable"), he would have been content to accept her in her differences from him. Surrealist love is spontaneous and cannot be chosen. It was not given to Breton to love Nadja:

Everything that enables a person to live on the simple life of another, without ever wanting to obtain from him more than he gives, that makes it sufficient just to see him moving or still, speaking or silent, waking or asleep, did not exist, had never existed: that was only too certain. It could not have been otherwise, considering Nadja's world, where everything so quickly took on the appearance of rising and falling. But I am judging *a posteriori* and I am taking a risk in saying it could never be otherwise. Whatever might have been my desire, or possibly my illusion, I was not up to what she suggested to me. (p. 127)

The blank space left in the text between the paragraph where Breton admits his possible shortcomings, a paragraph which ends with a construction patently contrary to fact: "only love . . .

could have permitted in this case the bringing about of the miracle," and the beginning of the next paragraph is in itself tragic. Without that miracle, there can never be communication between the "normal" world and the other, even for a Surrealist— "They came, some months ago, to tell me that Nadja was insane."

Nadja, unlike the "normal" Surrealists, has no instinct to call her back from the precipice, does not know the meaning of the expression *se tenir bien*.

Now I never imagined that she might lose or might already have lost the *help* of that instinct of conservation—to which I have already referred—and which means that, after all, my friends and I *behave ourselves,* for example, when a flag passes—limiting our action to turning our heads away. . . . (p. 136)

For those who "pass to the other side of the mirror" Breton has a genuine respect—which does not prevent him from remaining on this side. Nadja's conception of the proof of love was to rush head-long to their death together, with Breton at the wheel of the car, blinded by her hands over his eyes. She was capable of a *total* subversion of the life instinct, and whereas in retrospect, Breton admits the validity of such a test for friendship and for love ("Ideally at least I often find myself blindfolded at the wheel of this wild car," p. 44), it is undeniable that at this time he refused it. Would he have accepted, being in love?

The question at the end of this section—"Who goes there?"— is posed by Breton to himself, and he calls it an "always pathetic" cry. "Who goes there? Is it you, Nadja? Is it true that the *beyond* is in this life? I cannot hear you. Who goes there? Is it only I? Is it myself?" (p. 138) The book could have ended with this question as the only echo for the opening question; Nadja could have been only an exteriorization of the risk of Surrealism, made explicit and then eliminated. Yet in the last few pages, Breton begins again, not with a self-questioning but with an affirmation of the Surrealist manner of living life breathlessly, with a new sense of every moment, even those between the printed words in a sentence. Every sentiment here is turned to the positive, so that the silence is no longer seen, like the space between two worlds and the two paragraphs just mentioned, as a solitude, but as a space for miraculous change, from "myself" to the next "present sense of myself." Breton repeats the Surrealist credo in the unconscious, in uncertainty, in impatience, and in risk, as a balance (deliberate or unconscious?) for the more conservative passages on social behavior:

Nonetheless if one has to wait, to wish for certainty, to take precautions, to clear a particular space for the fire and only a particular space,[4] I refuse completely. Let the great unconscious, in all its vitality and reverberation, the unconscious which inspires my only convincing acts, dispose forever of all that I am. I remove from myself for no reason any opportunity to take back what I am once again granting. (p. 146)

The strength of this *irrational* vow and imprudent behavior compensates for whatever timidity and reserve we might have sensed in the comparison between Breton and Nadja, a comparison which he was at least honest enough to make.

However we may feel about Nadja's final replacement by the next incarnation of the free spirit (*"génie libre"*), we cannot deny that the ending is a strong one, as the woman loved gives to the already determined conclusion about the convulsive beauty its "true sense and all its force." Breton affirms his faith in the uniqueness of love as it puts an end to all the puzzling self-examinations ("Who am I?") and to the anguish of solitude ("Is it only I?"):

All I know is that the substitution of persons stops with you, because nothing can be substituted for you, and that for me this succession of enigmas was always destined to stop in front of you.
You are not an enigma for me.
I say that you turn me away forever from the enigma. (p. 151)

This last gesture Nadja could never have made. She was herself the mystery and pointed only to the mystery. That Breton should have preferred the nonenigma or the transcendence of enigma to the embodiment of enigma is perhaps not surprising from a human viewpoint, even if one would have drawn other conclusions from the precepts of Surrealism. Not only is it a great proof of humility, but it incorporates the ironies and the dualities which give to Surrealism its characteristic tone.

After all his self-examination, Breton concludes that the final *saccade* of beauty has all the importance which he would rather not give to himself. And after all the lyricism of language and the "marvelous" of anecdotes and strange events, he invokes their opposites: "Kingdom of silence . . ." (p. 154). Parallel to the image of the self-destructive couple in the car, the final image of the plane with which all communication is cut off is an example perhaps of convulsive beauty, and certainly of enigma. We may suspect that the plane does not crash and that the pilot is accompanied (Breton having said that the woman by his side in the car could have been any other as well as Nadja, and even a "certain other person"), but we cannot be sure. There is just as much distance between us and the plane as there was between Breton and the insane asylum, and perhaps this distance still remains between him and the pilot. "A morning newspaper will always suffice to bring me news of myself" (p. 154), which is entirely as it should be in a Surrealist novel. Any questions asked at the end are finally as much ours as they are the author's.

II   Les Vases communicants—(*1932*)

Maintenant que je ne la cherche plus, il m'arrive de la rencontrer quelquefois. Elle a toujours les yeux aussi beaux, mais il faut bien reconnaître qu'elle a perdu pour moi son prestige. (Now that I am no longer looking for her, I happen to meet her sometimes. Her eyes are still just as beautiful, but I have to admit that she no longer seems marvelous to me, *Les Vases communicants,* p. 111.)

Surrealism, in Breton's view, is primarily a unifying force. Against all separations and specializations it poses its single most important visual image, the communicating vessels already perceived in *Le Surréalisme et la peinture* of 1928. The volume which takes the name of the image is the indispensable document of this particular conception as well as of the links with and the differences from the Marxist theory.

At the center of the book Breton gives a definition of Surrealism far more lasting than was the often quoted definition in the first manifesto about automatism:

I hope that it stands as having tried nothing better than laying down a *conductor*[5] between the far too separated worlds of waking and sleeping, of exterior and interior reality, of reason and madness, of the calm of knowledge and of love, of life for life and the revolution, etc.

And then, since this is a defense of Surrealism against the accusation of its nonparticipation in the social revolution, Breton adds with characteristic feeling:

At least we will have tried, tried in vain perhaps but tried, not to leave any question without an answer and we will have cared about the consistency of the answers we gave. Supposing this terrain to have been ours, was it really of so little merit that we should have abandoned it? (p. 116)

The book, divided into three parts, does not give the same impression of willed disorder as *Nadja*. In the first part, Breton makes an ingenious and even a convincing case for linking imagination to action, and the time and space of the dream to those of the material world. In the second, he illustrates by personal experiences the workings of objective chance and the place of human love in the revolution against the bourgeois world as it stands. And in the third, he discusses the future relationship of the individual poet to the revolution and to other men.

The fact that *Les Vases communicants* has a slightly more "ordered" form does not invalidate the image of the swinging door found in *Nadja*. Here Breton only modifies that image to make it a half-open door between the imagined to the lived "or, more exactly, to the ought-to-live," so that it takes just one step to leave the "shaky house of poets and to find oneself on a level with life itself."

It has so far not been to the advantage of "literary people" to investigate the relationship between the two worlds, because they have claimed although wrongfully, as their property the revelations of dream. What is worse, they have exalted dream over action as a socially conservative device, since those who would be tempted to make revolutions can be persuaded instead to dream, safely. As for the professional psychologists (the *"last"* of the sciences") who should have taken a more responsible position, they have simply pushed "to the new shore, with beetle-like gestures, the ball of not very pertinent opinions that they have been rolling in front of them from the beginning of time" (p. 15). There is even a danger that the dream enigma be turned by some of them into the "most cretinizing religious mystery." From the standpoint of its emphatically antireligious position as well as its insistence on the abolition of any separation between "specializations," Surrealism is most decidedly humanistic. All the beginning pages of this volume lead up to the statement in the final part that man is the center of the universe and the only possible location for the resolution of its contradictions. For the Surrealists, belief in God and the future life is an obvious reduction of the importance of man and his imagination, and of the present life which must be changed, rather than transcended. So far the commentators on dream have neglected to indicate "on which side of the barricade they put themselves." Freud himself did not go far enough in his conclusions, since he separated "psychic reality" from "material reality," refused the prophetic dream dealing with the immediate future, and did not apply the full extent of his investigations to his own case. Breton calls this a *desertion* like any other.

The lengthy interpretation of his own dreams which follows in the first part (using the method of interpretation Freud gave) is to be seen as an example of the continuous mental activity taking place during sleep. It is exactly balanced in the second part (which opens with Breton recounting his dreams to Eluard, who serves as the listener of psychoanalytic sessions)[6] by a long account of Breton's daily life, which he convincingly describes as resembling the structure of a dream, and its illogical but marvelous atmosphere:

No sooner is one character seen than he is dropped for another—and, who knows, even for another? So then what is the point of all this exposition? The author seemed to be telling us something about his life, but he speaks as if in a dream! *As if in a dream* (p. 102)[7]

The autobiographical analysis here is the exact counterpart of the dramatic analysis in the first part; a series of coincidences, sentences which come "spontaneously" to mind and are commented on and interpreted, change linkings and recurrences (for example, of the names Olga, Samson, Batifol, etc.) exemplifying the Sur-

realist belief in objective chance, similar to the theory of Engels
which Breton quotes: "Causality can only be understood in connection with the category of objective chance, a particular form of
the manifestation of necessity" (p. 124). From all of this there
are two implied conclusions. First, that the structure of the dream
and of reality closely resemble each other, the marvelous and the
human mind demonstrating in both realms the same sorts of
function. Second, that love is an agent of perfection and of knowledge as well as of *folie*—and even an agent of nonidealization,
since gradually it progresses toward the *specific*.

On the purely choreographic level, the intertwining of the communicating vessels into the "unity of the materialist world" balances the recurring stress on Breton's position (or disposition) of
solitude ("the reconstitution of myself") throughout his various
attractions and disillusions, the split between his experiences with
their marvelous realizations of coincidence and his observations of
"average" life ("massive, not very productive, but at least indisputable," p. 113). The Sunday crowds by the river could never
share the intensely charged atmosphere of drama he inhabits:

I imagined without the least trace of irony all that was indissoluble,
facile between them. Two by two, they had chosen each other, one
day in haste, and there was no more question of their being able to
separate. No second thoughts. . . . The need to understand the world
a bit, the concern of differentiating oneself from other men, the hope
of helping to resolve a non-resolved thing, this motive at once stimulat-
ing and deceptive did not enter into it at all. Still it is for these people
that strawberries grow in the woods! (pp. 12–13)

While affirming that it is too late for him to resemble them in any
way, Breton thinks their position a privileged one "up to a certain
point." Read rapidly, this seems a sort of colonialist posture—the
natives have their advantages too, the simple life is tempting, but
on another level from ours, and so on. The isolated hero ("I re-
peat I was alone") expresses a genuine modesty about the human
situation in which he participates: "How does one go about simply
being a man?" To justify the place one occupies by intellectual
accomplishments[8] is far more difficult than to do so by physical
labor, for instance (here again, the facility of the primitive is taken

for granted). The intellectual comradeship he so often underlines (*"mes amis et moi"*) takes the place of that communication of spirit in the Sunday crowds. Ideally it should fill in the rift between Breton and those whose destiny is different, easier, as the rift between the two conceptions of Revolution is ideally resolved at the end of the book when outside communicates with inside, poets with "the others," light with dark, and dream with reality.

Breton's goal in this book is plainly one of resolution, of uniting what is now separate. The dream must be replaced "in its real framework which is none other than human life" (p. 29) as a demonstration that the supposed split between conscious thought and "total repose" is not only illusory but harmful, since the exiling of man into the nonconscious every night tends to make him "dangerously spiritualize" his own consciousness. Whereas the dream is a potential liberating force, mystifications easily attach to it; and they are antipathetical to the free spirit.

The major theme of the connection between dream and reality recurs, particularly in the first and third parts, in various formulations and accompanied by various images. The most successful of the latter is probably that of the capillary tissue lying between the two realms, assuring a constant interchange between the exterior and interior worlds, objective knowledge and subjective sentiment, the waking and the sleeping being. Man is, Breton claims, the mediator between two worlds, and it is in his "universal subjectivity" that all contradictions are dialectically resolved. The most general aim of Surrealism, as Breton now states it, is to go beyond the simple joining of elements to each other (which was its starting point and continues to determine its esthetics and its stylistics) in order to modify the role of man himself. Surrealism intends "to replace man at the heart of the universe, to take him away for a second from his disintegrating adventure, to remind him that he is for all sadness and all joy exterior to him an infinitely perfectible place of resolution and echo" (p. 28). According to him, the step to revolution is far easier to make from this position than from the traditional attitude of man as knower or learner. While objective knowledge is likely to teach cynicism, desire refuses itself nothing. "Resignation is not written on the moving stone of sleep."

Not only does the *"pur décor"* of the exterior world cut off all

the imaginative realities and the countless possibilities glimpsed in
the world of sleep, but its temporal structure imposes a "limitless
slavery" on us: "the search for concrete, continuous, immediate
efficacity. . . . This time I live in, this time unhappily ebbs away,
taking me with it" (p. 183). One has not so much here the sense
of Surrealist longing for an atemporal paradise as an actual impatience with the present moment ("insane impatience . . . is not
spared me," p. 183). Breton feels it significant that the cloud of
his particular epoch "draws its shadow over the page I write; let
this tribute be paid to the plurality in which, in order to dare to
write, I must at once lose and find myself" (p. 184). Only beyond the shadow of this cloud (which represents in this case the
economic regime of capitalism) can a person presume to give play
to his more individual feelings. In short, the impatience can be
defined as wanting to "hasten the hour of the Revolution," when
the human mind, freed from the more ignoble material wants, will
be "carried to a higher level" (p. 186).

And here the split between Surrealist thinking and traditional
Marxist thinking is clarified, or better, illuminated in its own
ambiguity. The shadow cast on the page once acknowledged, the
faith in a (permanent) revolution once stated, the subject of the
verb "write" emerges as more important than it might have
seemed before. Breton has justified the study of self only in terms
of "being able to integrate it with the collective being," but after
losing oneself in the plurality of voices, the individual voice finds
itself once more stronger than they are:

Who is to say if it is not appropriate that in the most tormented epochs,
the solitude of a few beings should deepen *in spite of themselves,*[9]
beings whose role is to prevent the disappearance of what subsists
ephemerally only in a corner of the greenhouse, to find much later its
place in the center of the new order, marking thus with a flower
absolutely and simply present, because it is *true,* of a flower in some
sense *axial in relation to the time,* that tomorrow be linked all the
more closely to yesterday, for having to break off more decisively
from it. (p. 187)

Breton wills himself a revolutionary, but he cannot will himself
one of the present masses. He calls for action, but it is to some
extent circumscribed within the realm of magic, "in the sense that

it consists in the unconscious immediate reaction of the internal
on the external, and that there slides easily into the final analysis
of such a notion the idea of a transcendent mediation which is
nearer to that of a demon than to that of a god" (p. 199).

Yet the most interesting sorts of ambiguity are revealed not
within the content, but rather within the style. Magic may be
considered an "immediate" action, but the final passage of the
book is in the lyric future, the privileged tense of the Surrealists,
who often substitute for Apollinaire's *"il y a"* an *"il y aura."* "The
poet to come will rise above the depressing idea of irreparable
divorce between action and the dream" (p. 198). Breton is not
describing, and *could not describe,* the poetic work at the moment
when he pictures its final emergence into broad daylight, so that
the "hair streaming with light" which he attributes to truth appears
at the "black window," thus uniting the brightness and the shadow.
He has already gone beyond the cloud over the written page and
even beyond the moment in which it will be swept away, into a
state of pure lyricism.

Beside all the other ambiguities felt in Breton's work there is
this most tragic one (or, in another perspective, most touching
one) which seems to predominate over all the rest: Surrealist
poetry wills itself present, but its entire feeling is future. The
constant refusal to foresee an *end* to revolution is not just a
theoretical refusal; it is also temperamental. The declaration at the
beginning of *Les Vases communicants* about "those who have
judged once and for all that after so many interpretations of the
world it is time to pass to its transformation" (p. 99) places only
the passing over in the present moment; the transformation is
marked as belonging to the continuous future. Some may consider this split between the poet of the present and his vision of
the future as a final, unconscious alienation of man from his action,
of his vision from our reality, and as a confirmation of the tenuous
quality of the communication between vessels of any sort. The
perspective from which one considers this particular text depends,
perhaps more than in the case of any other of Breton's texts, on
the distance one acknowledges (or allows) between poetry and
life. Breton himself more and more considered any such acknowl-
edgment as a compromise—it is in the light of his uncompromising
attitude that the text takes on its full tragic and heroic depth.

There is today little place, it is true, for anyone who would like to
trace, haughtily in the grass, the skillful arabesques of the suns. . . .
(p. 183)

III   L'Amour Fou (*1937*)

J'aimerais que ma vie ne laissât après elle d'autre murmure que celui
de guetteur, d'une chanson pour tromper l'attente. (I should like
my life to leave after it no other murmur than that of the watchman,
a song to while away the waiting, *L'Amour fou*, p. 33.)

The change of emphasis from *Les Vases communicants* to
L'Amour fou is unmistakable, from the will to collective revolutionary action to the acceptance of the *"comportement lyrique"* or
the poetic behavior of a smaller group. There are nuances to this
change; for instance, even in *Les Vases communicants,* the actual
split between the Surrealist idea of revolution and that usually
attributed to the Communist party is evident, as well as that between Breton as an individual and the many he observes, and
even in *L'Amour fou,* Breton continues to claim that the rule of
capitalism complicates the difficulties of unique love. He observes, in *L'Amour fou,* that the earlier work was "limited" by
his not having wanted to cut himself off from "practical action"
at that time; since he says, the passage from words to actions was
in fact not permitted to him, he finds himself free to re-examine
the questions of dream, of chance, and of desire.

The main requirement of this now fully accepted lyrical or
Surrealist behavior (Breton specifically equates the two) is that the
known should not be overestimated in relation to the unknown.
Dreams cannot be completely analyzed at a time contemporary
with them, because they have to remain open to the future; like
Breton's own "Tournesol," poems cannot be fully satisfying in
their properly predictive role until their full significance is seen
developing its own justification, which was once invisible to us.
Breton regrets the changes he made in this poem to render it
more "pleasing" and less obscure. (The regret is certainly justified, even from the purely "esthetic" point of view in which Surrealist work is not supposed to be judged although, ironically,
Breton's own work is unquestionably "satisfactory" by the most
exigent and enlightened esthetic standards.) Once its predictive

elements had been realized, the corrections instantly appeared retrospectively as *faults* of vision.

Surrealism sees the world as a forest of *indices,* or analogical indications, but it considers them far more dynamic and more revolutionary in their implications than the Baudelairean correspondances, as has already been suggested. The *insolite,* or the necessarily unusual appearance of things indispensable to Surrealist vision, is not easily accepted, even by Breton, nor is the fact that the exterior world seems to arrange itself for the benefit of the (unconscious) desire of the individual, whose responsibility it is always to remain open to the workings of chance. The Surrealist leap of faith is in every case accompanied by an inner doubt, essential to its particular character as is the distance between the two poles of the Surrealist image to the force of that image. "I hesitate, I have to admit, to make this leap, I am afraid of falling into the unlimited unknown" (p. 47).

The *"insolite"* and the *"faits-précipices"* which embody it are a definite cause of fear, and at the same time, the clearest example of the marvelous junctions which Breton makes the centers of his books, the "necessary" communications between men and things, the mental and the material, the subjective and the objective, in short, the frequent manifestations near to us of the *point sublime* which is never quite within our reach. Most of the Surrealist games are directed at creating the greatest possible number of these junctions—for example, the game of definitions, where the participants have no idea of the object which they are defining. Re-creations of language, revision of the standard purpose of things, multiplication of images, which are only instruments capable of forcing the universe to give up its opacity for an only partially obscured clarity: these are the goals of Surrealist play.

Both in the place they occupy and the importance Breton attaches to them, the two central images of this book are privileged. The locomotive stopped at its greatest speed in a virgin forest represents the perfect junction of mobility and immobility— Breton calls it a monument "to victory and to disaster" (p. 76). An example of convulsive beauty (whose sexual implications are clear), it represents an ideal and permanent state of what is in ordinary life a transient rapidity of movement, as well as its destruction "in the exact moment of its expiration." The image which is its counterpart in the constantly balanced structure of Surrealism is the far more famous one of the crystal, also implying the perfection of motion stilled (here Breton refers to Hegel). Concentrated into a smaller space than the first image and therefore carrying an even greater potential force, the crystal is the guiding image of many Surrealist works. A combination of complexity (in its facets) and simplicity of form, of the clarity and the spontaneous hardness both Dada and Surrealism oppose to the laborious *work* and the weak sentimentality of bourgeois taste and morality, the crystal is the ultimate Surrealist aspiration: "the key to the fields lies in the crystal." [10]

"Love with its retinue of clarities," "this chain of illuminations passing through us," love "as an apparatus of mirrors," "enabling us to create a diamond from the blackest of nights": [11] of all the perfect condensations and marvelous junctions, human love is the most crystalline for Breton. By its nature it refuses any separation between man and the world of nature, so that Breton can identify the woman he loves with "the snow of mountain peaks at sunrise." The miraculous embodiment of dizziness (*"le vertige"*) and the odd mobile/immobile permanence of convulsive spontaneous beauty, irrational Surrealist love is mad (*"fou"*) in its complete freedom from the limits of logic and from the nuances and vicissitudes of intellect. But inescapably, the theme of human judgment enters. *L'Amour fou,* which ends with Breton's hope that his little daughter be "madly loved" and which takes as its motif the positive value of such love, begins with a disquisition on variations, on the procession of beings loved and of the "selves" that loved them, as if, seen in the most trivial light, this sort of preface indicated a conscience not at rest with itself (or, in fact, the sense of malediction of which Breton speaks here). One would choose to have loved only one being, and yet all the successive figures Breton imagines seated on two facing benches and judging him represent unique moments of sincere conviction. He has been all those past images of himself and he has loved all those corresponding images; the synthesis he longs for is attainable only if all the past beings were prefigurations of the present one, who is in all senses ultimate. Parallel to this solution of synthesis is one of multiplication. As the various are one, so the one is various:

Because you are unique, you cannot fail to be always another in my
eyes, another you. Across the diversity of these inconceivable flowers,
over there in the distance, changeable, it is you whom I love in a red
gown, in a grey gown. (p. 92)

This repetition which he likens to that of one single plant growing
always taller, is (like the crystal, like the art of the insane, and like
the word "always") a "key to the limitless fields."

But at the moment of grace, just when the synthesis is to be
realized, Breton undergoes a mental crisis of confidence in himself,
parallel to the doubt he felt before at exposing himself to the
indispensable perils of the *insolite:*

Of what am I finally capable? What shall I do in order not to be
unworthy of such a fate? . . . All sorts of defenses become visible
around me, clear bursts of laughter come from the past to finish in
sobs, under the great beatings of grey wings in an uncertain spring
night. . . . Who goes with me at this hour in Paris without guiding me
and whom, moreover, I am not guiding? I don't remember ever having
felt such a weakness. I become almost invisible to myself. (p. 53)

And, accompanied by the woman desperately loved in what should
be a profoundly marvelous and above all, genuine, moment,
Breton feels the moment threatened by the same sense of the artificial which had eventually ruined Nadja's words for him: "The
conversation . . . only touches the mask of things. Now I am
frightened to feel myself leading it against my will toward the
artificial" (p. 54). Only in stories does doubt never creep in.
Here his heightened sensitivity only aggravates the pessimism of his
vision and, in a state of uncertainty corresponding to the cloudy
spring night, he echoes once more his questioning at the beginning
of *Nadja* (*"Qui suis-je?"*):

I see the bad and the good in their crudest state, the bad winning out
by all the ease of suffering. Life is slow and man hardly knows how
to play it. . . . Who goes with me, who goes in front of me once again
tonight? . . . There is still time to turn back. (p. 54)

But all the uncertainty and suffering do finally contribute to the
Surrealist idea of *"l'amour fou."* As Breton explains to his daughter at the end, the night of the "Tournesol" would have been far

less radiant without the preceding misery, as the notion of the crystal, in Surrealism, always includes obscurity. That may perhaps seem a facile, or at least obvious, resolution of the difficulty. What is more interesting is that this moment of hesitation and even anguish while Breton and his future wife are walking about in Paris is exactly paralleled by another such moment while the two of them are walking down a Brittany shore. During the latter, a serious, *irrational* irritation overcomes Breton, and though he later explains it by the proximity of a malevolent object (in this case a particular house, which is in its turn parallel to an "evil mask previously mentioned), the "explanation" does not change the fact that the moment exists as a *hole* in the "chain of illumination" which it has interrupted. It is not too strong to say that Breton is obsessed with *discontinuity,* of which all the images of arrested motion are only the positive side, and that they are balanced by others, more threatening: "The mirror clouds over . . ." (p. 135).

Breton proclaims, in describing the *point sublime* at the close of the book, that he has only wanted to know the triumphal hours of love, and maintains that his own occasional incapacity or lack of faith subtracts nothing from the great hope that he places in "l'amour fou." Surrealist love, since it is still a human love, includes the moments of necessary despair inflicted by the universe, but is in no way defeated by them: "I do not deny that love is at odds with life. I say it must win, and that in order to do so, it must be raised to such a poetic consciousness of itself that everything it meets which is necessarily hostile to it will melt in the hearth of its own glory" (p. 135). To his faith in the continuous and the multiple—the faith that the women loved includes not only all the past women loved, but is herself many women—this fear of the discontinuous is an echo. Seen in another light, it seems a complementary faith: that the hope of Surrealism itself lies in the definitive novelty of each new moment. "Tomorrow will be another, completely torn off from yesterday." Befitting the drama of Surrealism, this is in no way a tranquil faith, but a violent one: "torn off" (*"déchiré"*). The resolution of these faiths takes place in Surrealist love as it is expressed in one of the most famous of all Surrealist lines: "Always for the first time."

The convulsive beauty mentioned at the end of *Nadja* and perfectly corresponding in a positive sense to the opening uncertainty, takes on an additional complexity here, almost ten years later. The permanence of discontinuity, like the arresting of violent motion at the moment of its expiration, creates an exceptional intensity within each moment, an intensity so great that, against all the rational warnings of the outside world, it does not permit the prediction of any decadence, or any degradation in time. Regardless of all *variations,* when Breton speaks of the battle between the notions of "forever" and "for a long time," he shows no hesitation:

Of these words, the one that carries my colors, even if its star is on the decline, even if it must lose, is *always.* . . . What I have loved, whether I have kept it or not, *I shall love always.* (p. 134)

The irrationality of Surrealist love will save it from the cautions of reason. Nadja, in her extreme of irrationality, was not saved; yet who is to say that her aloneness did not always haunt Breton, not only in his moments of doubt ("Who goes with me?"), but also in his moments of faith? For a certain loneliness pierces through the optimism even when Breton is defining love as a union of two beings in a prelogical state of grace, and it can be interpreted, like his self-questioning, as an echo of her own:

. . . the fusion restores to all things the lost colors of the time of ancient suns, where, however, solitude also rages . . . (p. 10).

IV   Arcane 17 (*1944*)

Une lacune dans le rêve. Est-ce à dire que rien n'est jamais retrouvé? mais cette certitude désolante en appelle aussitôt une autre qui la compense, mieux même, qui est capable de concilier l'esprit avec la première, et cette certitude seconde c'est que rien n'est jamais perdu. (A gap in the dream. Does it mean that nothing is ever found again? but this distressing certainty calls immediately for another to compensate for it, even better, to reconcile the mind with the first, and this second certainty is that nothing is ever lost, *Arcane 17,* p. 144.)

Nadja opened with a question of identity, *Les Vases communicants* with a meditation on the dream; *Arcane 17* opens with a straightforward statement where both are assumed, and neither discussed: "In Elisa's dream. . . ." A "real" woman and the "real" landscape of the Gaspé Peninsula form the background for the book, in which the soliloquy on anarchy and on the true "adventures of the mind" (those who refuse both *"le pli"* of traditions and the patina of institutions) takes second place to the descriptions of love as a perfect union of existence and essence. It is now for Breton the profound and all-inclusive human counterpart of the sublime point and the marvelous image, a union so luminous that either of its elements seen without the other "appears to be the result of a dissociation, a dislocation of one single block of light" (p. 39).

Arcane 17, a book in praise of the esoteric, is nevertheless filled with images of light, transparency, incandescence ("this luminous point," p. 19; "incandescent points," p. 22; "this flame," "the window unveils itself," p. 121; "all the lights prepare to communicate," p. 75), these befitting Breton's rediscovery of personal happiness and a concurrent faith in the possible "Resurrection" of all things from their state of melancholy and apparent death:

Yes, the highest thoughts, the noblest feelings can experience a collective decline, and also the human heart can break and books can get old and everything must die on the exterior, but a power in no sense supernatural makes even of this death the condition for renewal. It guarantees as a preliminary all the exchanges which see to it that nothing precious is lost on the interior, and that through the obscure metamorphosis, from season to season, the butterfly will take on again his exalted colors. (pp. 128–29)

Even the stagnant pond described in these pages comes to life as the waves sweep across it. This is the poetic faith, and Breton assures us that its true place is never *in* the world, but somewhat removed from the place of action, that the "fields of discovery" (these fields to which he so often refers) are interior. The Resurrection, like the Rebellion he encourages, carries its justification *in itself* and cannot be disappointed by events extrinsic to it. The latter, insofar as the world is influenced by what Breton calls the "masculine mind" in its rational state, can only be redeemed by the fertile *anima* or the irrational feminine mind as it is expressed in poetry and art. Here Breton states his faith in a "terrestrial salvation by woman."

In the face of the intransigence of the rational which has produced the most sterile and the cruelest of worlds, Breton invokes her always powerful cry of "refusal and alarm," her insistence on the brotherhood of man and her warning about the dangers of nationalism. For him, woman is at once the Morning Star ("the star is upon you"), Lucifer the Light-Bearer, Eve, and the individual woman illuminating the individual man: "When fate brought us together, the greatest shadow was in me and I can say that it is within me that this window was opened" (p. 105). Above all she is Mélusine. Both mermaid and woman, child and adult, sister to the alchemists and their ideal mistress, Mélusine in her marvelously dual nature is the heroine of the most "splendid myth" of Surrealism. "I choose the child-woman, not to oppose her to the other woman, but because in her and only in her does the other prism of vision seem to dwell in absolute transparency" (p. 198).[12] In spite of all the magical transformations, she is always like herself, she proves the permanence of the miracle: "For Mélusine, before and after the metamorphosis, *is* Mélusine" (p. 92).

From his ideal point on the Rocher Percé (though he takes pains to state that "everything" prevents him from being, even there, the ideal observer), Breton salutes not only the double nature of woman and the extraordinary luminosity of human love in spite of its myriad deceptions, but the more general "fragility" and "magnificence of the human gift." Finally he invokes the alchemical work (or the *arcane work*) which touches the poetic genius and the poetic life in its *play* of opposites ("this atrocious emptiness replacing without the least transition the fullness of the heart"), which the dual nature of Mélusine perfectly fits. The hidden regions where the alchemical work transforms the opposites into a crystalline union can be explored only by poetry, and only the poet aided by his *soror* has access to them, for it is in her eyes that they are completley revealed. In describing his mental anguish and his struggle to "recover the poetic understanding of the universe beyond the great pity of the epoch and my own confusion," Breton pays the highest possible tribute to the woman whose "grandeur" saved him from despair. He is able now to reiterate his faith in "love, but only as between two beings it rises to the invulnerable," in art, "but only art in its supreme solicitations and the struggle to the bitter end for liberty" (p. 81).

Arcane 17 is not a retreat from the image of *Les Vases communicants,* but its double. At a certain point of the day, Breton remarks, "It is done: all the lights communicate" (p. 76).

CHAPTER 9

Poetry: "Lieu de reconciliation"

I   Reading a Surrealist Poem*

Indication A: Surrealism is based on contrast of will and perception: the will to *link* and the constant perception of *contraries*. It is the tension between these two elements which furnishes the energy and the basis for Surrealist poetry.

Indication B: This tension is reflected in the individual verses, first by the necessary distance between the two elements of the image, since the Surrealists accept Reverdy's celebrated dictum according to which it is always their polarity that creates the momentum for the shock of the image. And secondly, these images are themselves put into a succession of images so that their horizontal tension is part of a prolonged tension (or sustained shock) as one reads down the page (or listens to the poem read in the order of its parts). The images may seem to build a series of descriptions less shocking than successive and cumulative. But unless the over-all impression is as much one of contrary perceptions as of linking, the poem is probably not successful as a Surrealist poem. Although the feeling, or tension, of a Surrealist poem cannot always be described (that is, one cannot always say: this represents a tension between A and B), the reader must be in some fashion aware of it; and the more accustomed one is to reading Surrealist poetry, the more one develops a certain sensitivity to that particular tension and to that kind of linking.

Indication C: Surrealism is less an individual attitude than that of a group; a Surrealist poem is often better seen in its relations with other Surrealist poems than alone. Like the elements of the image, Surrealist poems can be placed side by side and statements made about them with that juxtaposition as a starting point which can then be applied to the individual poems themselves.

Application: as an experiment, on the basis of these three indica-

---

*See Appendix.   **87**

tions, let us take for example just the images of three poems from the collection *L'Air de l'eau,* the poems beginning: "L'aigle sexuel exulte," "Il allait être cinq heures," and "Ils vont tes membres." In all three poems, the predominating images are of wings (of an eagle, of the woman loved), of clarity (clear days, a glass newspaper, a mirror, an electric light, sunbeams, window panes and glaziers, water, a prismatic bed), of the color green (mint, emerald, foliage and particular leaves, green eyebrows and green sheets, a willow), and of a sense of danger (an incision, scars, the loss of leaves and the ripping of the veins from a leaf, a leaf slippery and with no edges, saws, a dagger, blood).

The links between one image and another can be seen as evident and implied, on the level of vision (a), of imagination (b), and of word play (c): from the bright and liquid air in the first poem to the liquid wing in the third, from window panes in the first and second poems to the window pane makers (glaziers) in the third (a); from the sexual image at the opening of the first poem to the bifurcation and the mingling of the blood in the second, to the three references to the bed in the third (b); from the word *"manches"* (sleeves) in the first poem to the *"manche"* (handle) of the dagger in the second, and from the *"verre"* (glass) to the *"ver luisant"* (glowworm) in the second poem to the *"draps verts"* (green sheets) in the third (c).

The contrasts and tensions seem inseparable from the linking. In the first poem a descending and an ascending wing are joined in two successive lines, and death and life are joined in the same line; similarly the images of cold (snow, icebergs, frozen particles in the first, and icicles in the second) contrast with the sexual images. In the second poem, falling and rising are opposed a few lines apart, while joy is apparent *in* the exhalation of grief, and the rustling of flowers and the icicles meet in the same line. Furthermore there is an implied and important opposition of the hermetic to the crystal-clear. Paradigmatic of the linking process which makes its own opposition to the oppositions already mentioned, the coral handle of the dagger which bifurcates, does so in order to join the blood of the lovers, and the coral, which may be of the same color as the blood. And in the last poem, the bell towers meet each other. The repetitions of certain words within the poems

serve as simple carriers for the association of imagery: *"son aile
. . . son aile," "au premier rayon, dans ce rayon," "un cri, un cri."*

Furthermore, the over-all "theme" of *L'Air de l'eau* or of each
of its poems individually can be interpreted as one of linking (for
example in the title: the air of water)—the linking of love, and the
sexual union of opposites, the relation between love and life, of
the clear air and the clear wing perceived *in spite of* the more
ominous linking of life, danger and death. The rise and fall of the
eagle's wings, the falling star and the diving bell rising, reflect the
positive rhythm of lovemaking as surely as they do the tragic
uncertainty of human fortunes: the dangerous and yet exalted
image of the dagger's bifurcation is the central one here. The
freshness of the images of clarity and of green indicates birth and
rebirth, as do the allusions to a Maternity hospital and, in the first
poem, to the dreams potential in each person loved and in the
imagination of the poet:

> Alors des étendues jettent l'ancre se déploient au
>   fond de mon oeil fermé
> (Then great expanses cast their anchor and range themselves
>   in the depths of my closed eye)

So that the possible horror of the "green sheets," which might have
been associated with mold, are more likely linked to the cycle of
rebirth; they are later compared to an almond, and the whole bed
takes on a marvelous prismatic transparency. Within the world of
Surrealist poetry, all things are probably true, and the only betrayal
is to *limit.*

Each of the poems ends with union. The first unites the poet
and the world; the second, the poet and the woman loved: the
third, where the bed/sailboat is then a liquid wing beating in the
song of the window makers (or, by extension, in the poetry of the
Surrealist), is thus a union of love and adventure, an exultation in
transformations and in clarity. Together, the poems reinforce each
other in their contrasts, their tensions, in their associations and
their conclusions—as should be the case with poems from the
same collection. But on a more general scale, all the most genuine
Surrealist poems can be considered as belonging to the same collection. Most of Breton's best poems, and those of the other

Surrealists, show the "Free Union" he extols between the poet and
the woman, between the poem and the universe it mirrors, between
the poet's perception and his representation. And this union is the
possible union of all his work, of the hermetic and the clear: "to
make the windows fly open."

II   "Puis la poésie aux phares rouges sur une mer toute brune"

For several reasons, Breton's poems should not be discussed in
isolation from one another; unlike ordinary "texts," they are wit-
nesses to the poetic spirit rather than examples of individual creation. Nor should they be separated from discussions of Breton's
"theories" as purely lyric statements. Surrealism is, or wills itself
to be, a unifying force, and such "lyricism" as there is cannot be
dissociated from Surrealist beliefs: they are linked with the *fil
conducteur* that runs through all Surrealist discourse, thought,
and practice. In Surrealism, nothing is superfluous, and within the
realm of Surrealist concern, all is of equal importance.

As an example of the linking between theory and poetry, one
could take the long and important *Ode à Charles Fourier;* within
this one poem it is an easy matter to find references, however
rapid, to almost all of the main Surrealist attitudes. Here Breton
rails against the "stupid anesthesia of flags," implying in that expression all the assembled menaces (from his point of view) of
nations, families, wars, religions, categories of every sort which
dull the instinct for the new and the unexplored. Here he attacks,
with Fourier, all the "immobilistic" thinkers who would prevent
the constant *motion* to which the Surrealists are committed; here
he insists on the value of the world of sleep, but refuses at the
same time to acknowledge the single utility of any one *lever* on
the machine, that is, of any one process or theory. He insists on
the ritual and the optimistic aspect of the *"sens de la fête"* (the
latter word including the several religious and secular meanings of
feast, celebration, festival) and on the necessity of maintaining
"the integrity of the word" (here also, the latter term has all its
religious connotations as well as the literary-verbal ones). But here
too Breton laments the necessary brevity of the *"images fugaces,"*
their essentially fleeting quality. The catalogue of theories directly
referred to or indirectly implied could be extended and the same

sort of catalogue could be drawn up for the other long poems such as *Les Etats-Généraux* and *Fata Morgana.*

The interpenetration of theory and poetic text can best be indicated not by separating poems by their particular emphasis, or by tracing their chronology, but by combining them in a way which assumes them to be of equal importance and of essential relevance, whatever their date or length.

III   "L'alphabet secret de la toute-nécessité" (*1940*)

Words, the word, language, the work of language: the intimate and constant connection between the alchemy of the word and the Surrealist endeavor has already been underlined. For the Surrealist, the word is eternally fascinating, in the strongest possible sense of the latter term:

> Le ventre des mots est doré ce soir et rien n'est
> plus en vain
> (The body of words is gilded tonight and nothing
> is any longer in vain—"Ligne Brisée")

Expression is thought—it is not an adjunct, or a transcription, or in any way to be considered subsequent to thinking. It is in some cases prior to thought, as in automatic writing, or supposed, in all but the most exceptional cases, to be contemporary with thought. Language is incantation: the very mention at the close of "Hôtel des étincelles" of a book inscribed with the words *No tomorrow* lends a retrospective horror to the entire poem, a horror prepared by the image of a "hellish window" in the third line. The sentiment seems to depend as much on the literal sight of the words as on their actual content. In a passage in *Fata Morgana* describing furniture heavier than if it were filled with the sand from the sea bottom, Breton calls for word-levers to be used in removing it, as if nothing and no one else would be strong enough for such a job. The uttering of the word is sufficient, as the simple vision of the imagination is not. Always, even after the initial enthusiasm of automatic writing had passed, Breton claimed that the vision came *after* the words which stated it. And he never ceased to insist on the perpetual possibility of *any* miracle which is solicited by speech:

Et pour une fois ne se peut-il que l'expression *pour la vie* déclenche
une des aurores boréales dont sera fait le tapis de table du Jugement
Dernier?

(And for once may not just the expression *for life* be enough to produce an aurora borealis like those of which the tablecloth of the Last
Judgment will be made?, p. 38)

The preceding example, which fuses the present, the future, and
the eternal, is taken from the collection *Clair de terre,* whose title
is another fusion of terms and of vision (*"clair de lune"* = moon-
light, so *"clair de terre"* = earthlight, to emphasize the non-
heavenly nature of the marvelous). Such fusions are also responsible for one title already discussed ("L'Air de l'eau") and
for the last line of the poem about a wild flame (*"flamme bar-
bare"*): "Flamme d'eau guide-moi jusqu'à la mer de feu (Flame of
water lead me to the sea of fire)." Surrealist language, for which
the Surrealist image is a model, is frequently a joining or "tele-
scoping" of partial or complete elements to make untried com-
pounds.

Doubling this *concentration* of language and thought is the
opposite process of expansion, whereby the mention of a term
provokes the mention of another in some way like it, and then
a series of images appropriate to both, in deliberate multiplications
of ambiguity and ramifications of the original simple vision or
expression. This process is so rapid as to create no sense of preci-
osity, only a series of what seem to be "marvelous" coincidences.
Thus a ruby leads to a rose which will lead to the similar sound
of dew (*"rosée"*), and any of these may lead to a fish called
"rouget" ("Au beau demi-jour," *L'Air*) as easily as the color rose
leads visually to the color red (*"rouge"*), or the sound "rose" to a
rose windodw (*"rosace"* in Hôtel des étincelles," *Le Revolver*).
Or a fistful of anything, similar to a handle by association of
meaning as well as sound (both are *"poignée"*) leads to the sword
which one grips (*"poignard"*) by simple repetition (*"Il allait
être cinq heures," L'Air*)—although the resulting poem is often a
complicated jigsaw puzzle in which the simplicity is apparently lost.
The quantities of puns (*"la mourre, l'amour," Les Etats-Généraux,
"le coeur m'en dit, le coeur mendie," "Toutes les écolierès en-
semble," Le Revolver*) and interior echoes such as those in

Breton's famous poem for his wife significantly entitled *L'Union libre ("aux mollets de modelle" "au cou d'orge . . . à la gorge . . . d'or")* develop into passages of a verbal richness which would cloy, were it not so brief, as the moods in Surrealist poetry are always shifting:

> Au dos de lumière
> À la nuque de pierre roulée et de craie mouillée
> Et de chute d'un verre dans lequel on vient de boire
>
> (Her back of light
> Her nape of crushed stone and moistened chalk
> And the fall of a glass from which one has
>   just finished drinking)

The visual-verbal references are more often subtle than the purely verbal ones, as for instance in one of the color-sound transferences already mentioned which comes from the same poem:

> Ma femme aux seins de creuset du rubis
> Aux seins de spectre de la rose sous la rosée
>
> (My wife with breasts of the crucible of ruby
> With breasts of the spectre of the rose under
>   the dew),

in which the color extends from the fire implied in the crucible to the rose lost (and haunting) under the dewdrops as the syllable "rose" haunts the word *"rosée."* Breton uses, perhaps unconsciously—which in no way invalidates or changes the tenor of that use—a whole range of references of this nature. The range stretches from a simple association and transfer, where the middle term is present by implication—for instance, the "lacerated curtains" lead to the "book scribbled in," by means of the ambiguity of the middle term *"griffé"* = scratched, like lacerated, and also scribbled ("Hôtel des étincelles," *Le Revolver*), and the chopping of a tree leads to the "cordes" of a musical instrument, by means of the middle term "cord of wood," the quantity you chop, a term absent but implied ("Les Attitudes spectrales," *Le Revolver*)—to the more complicated examples where the middle term or *mediator* is suppressed altogether:

La crêpe qu'il faut lancer si haut pour la dorer . . .
La crêpe magique le sceau aérien . . .
(The crêpe you have to flip so high to make it
    golden . . .
The magic crêpe the airy seal . . ., p. 81)

Here the word *"sceau"* is a homonym for the absent term *saut* (leap), associated with the tossing of the pancake into the air ("J'ai devant moi," *L'Air*).

There is the same range in vision, from the relatively simple analogy of form "net of roots" to "spider web" ("Sur la route qui monte et qui descend," *Le Revolver*), through the association by contrast and by potentiality (for instance, the description of the Indian chief, whom Breton calls the "rusted man in the machine," [1] up to the mood/sound/concept contrasts of the intricate and beautiful prose poem on despair called "Le Verbe être":

Je me lève chaque jour comme tout le monde et je détends les bras sur un papier à fleurs, je ne me souviens de rien et c'est toujours avec désespoir que je découvre les beaux arbres déracinés de la nuit. . . . Il fait un temps de temps.

(I get up every day like everyone else and I stretch out my arms on a floral wallpaper, I remember nothing and it is always with despair that I discover the beautiful uprooted trees of the night. . . . It is a weather of time, p. 86).

Here the optimism of the getting up and of the day contrast with the despair and with the nocturnal storm, as do the artificial prettiness and calm of the wallpaper, and yet the paper flowers are from a certain point of view uprooted from their "natural" surroundings as are the trees. The final mockery of our language echoes the despair and the sameness of the "every day" and the "everyone else," since a weather fit for dogs (*"temps de chien"*) or any such expression would have been less hollow than this weather which only repeats itself, (literally "weather of weather") as if the words were also "uprooted" from their sense.

Of course no word play or image play would be particularly significant were it not for Breton's absolute conviction that re-arrangements or re-creations of language and vision touch, not just language and vision, but the universe beyond them. His stubborn refusal to *separate* realms of activity confers on all those realms an equal importance—so that, finally, the mode of expression of one poem or all of Breton's poems, is no less serious than his ideas themselves.

IV "Le cristal noir"

Appositions of diametrically opposed elements are the basis for much Surrealist writing and for the "shock" of its style, whether it be spontaneous or deliberate. The contrasting images are not in themselves of an extreme intricacy, but form the basic and even simple structure which holds together the complexities of vision.

Although some of the contrasts are conceptual (ascending and descending wings, saved and lost, good and bad), some are slightly more complicated, combining the visual with the conceptual; for example, "le coup de revolver le sang qui saute lestement les marches vertes" ("the shot the blood skipping nimbly over the green steps"), where the implied wounding contrasts with the briskness of the motion and the red color with the green of the steps, the latter implying freshness, spring, and so on, and the red, both vitality and suffering or the passion of both, in an ambiguity of content as well as of vision. Or, to take another example, Breton's identification[2] of the woman with "Une haute flamme couchée dans la neige (A high flame lying in the snow)," so that the color of the flame contrasts directly with the white of the snow, as well as the heat with the cold, and the height with the horizontal position (as opposed to the perfectly simple contrasts like "le rayon se posa sur la fenêtre gelée/the sunbeam came to rest on the frozen window," p. 201).

But the great majority by far are oppositions of light and dark, clarity and shadow. Such oppositions reappear constantly in most of the poetry associated with Surrealism, and especially in that of Tristan Tzara and Paul Eluard; for any of these poets, one can make an almost endless catalogue of light/dark alternations, sometimes identified with rapid changes of mood, but sometimes a mere spectacle. In the following examples from Breton's poetry, to which many more could have been added, the obvious light/dark oppositions are underlined:

le soleil *blanc* et *noir*
(the white and black sun, p. 71)

ses lances *blanches* et *noires*
(its white and black lances, p. 227)

Une voiture *noire* rapide
Couronnée d'aigles de *nacre*
(A fast black car
Crowned with mother-of-pearl eagles, pp. 160–61)

Page de *brune* au béret de cendre *blanche* . . .
(Page of dusk with a beret of white ashes, "Le Volubilis et je sais
    l'hypotenuse")

Ici le temps *se brouille* à la fois et *s'éclaire*
(Here the weather clouds over and grows clear at the same time, p.
    189)

On dirait qu'on bat des cartes de *miroir* dans *l'ombre*
(You would think they were shuffling mirror cards in the shadow,
    p. 215)

Jersey Guernsey par temps *sombre* et *illustre*
(Jersey Guernsey in dark and shining weather, p. 218)

Est-ce l'amour ces doigts qui pressent la cosse du *brouillard*
Pour qu'en jaillissent les villes inconnues aux portes hélas *éblouissantes*
L'amour ces fils télégraphiques qui font de la *lumière insatiable* un
    brillant sans cesse qui se rouvre
De la taille même de notre compartiment de *la nuit*
Tu viens à moi de plus loin que *l'ombre* . . .
(Is it love these fingers pressing on the husk of the fog
To make the unknown towns alas with dazzling doors spring forth
Love these telegraphic wires that make of insatiable light a ceaseless
    diamond reopening
As large as our compartment of night
You come to me from farther off than shadow . . ., p. 186)

Sometimes a whole poem is entirely constructed around the alternation from light to dark, as is "Le Sphinx vertébral," which
opens with the shadow curved and patient hovering about the
paving stones and, after a few lines, switches to the scene of *"ce
matin, proue du Soleil"* ("this morning prow of the Sun"), where
the sense of adventure and movement is contrasted with the

slower-moving shadow. Now glaciers melt in a ray of light, and a wolf with glass (crystal) teeth is described growling at twilight and "smoking little fires" at night among the turnips. White birds appear, darkening a casement window by their flight, and laying black eggs. And finally, the poem moves in time from the simple juxtaposition of the two contraries:

> Il fait jour à gauche mais complètement nuit à droite
> (It is day on the left side but completely black
>   on the right side)

to the progress from one toward another seen at the end of the poem as the slow working of a primitive machine:

> Les guetteuses se penchent se penchent[3] aux
>   fenêtres
> De tout leur côté d'ombre de tout leur côté de
>   lumière
> La bobine du jour est tirée par petits coups
>   du côté du paradis de sable
> Les pédales de la nuit bougent sans interruption
>
> (The watchers lean lean at their windows
> From their whole side of shadow from their whole
>   side of light
> Bit by bit the bobbin of the day is pulled toward
>   the side of the paradise of sand
> The pedals of the night move without stopping, p. 102)

"Eclats de midi" ("bursts of noon"), *"Verres de lampes"* ("panes of the lamp"), *"Polis mes yeux"* ("my eyes polished"), *"O vitres superposés de la pensée/Dans la terre de verre"*[4] (Oh layered windowpanes of thought/In the glass earth): the ideal of Surrealism is undoubtedly one of radiance, illumination, of the crystal, of the marvelous. But it is not so simple as it might appear at first, and the very proliferation of the contraries is an indication of that. Here the alchemical lesson is invaluable, for it is within the dark that the light is to be found. Tzara declares in a *Note sur la poésie:* "Obscurity is productive if it is a light so white and pure that our neighbors are blinded by it,"[5] and Breton frequently associates sparks, mirrors, or even diamonds with shadow, dust, and

fog—*"Glace de ténèbres miroir d'amour"* ("Looking-glass of shadow mirror of love," p. 148); *"l'éclatante poussière"* ("the radiant dust," p. 214).

In a similar fashion, the transferences, fusions, and reversals effected during the alchemical work are characteristic also of Surrealist vision. The preferred Surrealist game is that of *"l'un dans l'autre"* (or one within the other), where the players accustom themselves to the *derivation* of objects from other objects in some way like them, the best example being the match which contains the lion in potentiality, because of the resemblance of the matchflame to the mane of the lion. Thus in Breton's poems, we see the forest (or the wood) *within* the hatchet, or, in another sort of transference, the bars on the inside of the cage. These *inversions* of vision are typically Surrealist, and they are, like the alternations and ambiguities of form, responsible in large part for the supposed difficulties of much Surrealist work. It is difficult in the sense that alchemical work is meant to be difficult: the uninitiated will stumble. But for the others—and only to the extent that a non-Surrealist is not doomed to be an eternal noninitiate—at least a partial illumination is possible.

V "Et mouvement encore"

In his "qualité de convulsionnaire," the Surrealist has an innate tendency toward adventure and toward danger. As convulsive beauty depends on the shock of contrast, on the deliberate and yet spontaneous tensions created for instance between great momentum and absolute paralysis, high speed and total rest, the sense of adventure depends at least partly on the danger/pleasure contrast. Inferior in number only to the contrasts of light and dark are those of luxury and suffering, voluptuousness and violence, similar to those found in the Gothic novel, to which the Surrealists are so attached:

> Le vrai luxe
> C'est que le divan capitonné de satin blanc
> Porte l'étoile de la lacération
>
> (Real luxury
> Is for the divan covered in white satin
> To carry the star of laceration, p. 173)

> D'un coup de baguette ç'avaient été les fleurs
> Et le sang

> (At a wave of the stick it was flowers
> And blood, p. 201)

There is no better example of this juxtaposition/identification than the poem entitled "Les Écrits s'en vont." Beginning with a voluptuous image (found also in Tristan Tzara's *L'Homme approximatif* of 1930):

> Des bras qui ne s'articulent à rien d'autre
>   qu'au danger exceptionnel d'un corps fait
>   pour l'amour
> Dont le ventre appelle les soupirs détachés des
>   buissons pleins de voiles
> Et qui n'a de terrestre que l'immense vérité
>   glacée des traineaux de regards sur l'étendue
>   toute blanche
> De ce que je ne reverrai plus
> A cause d'un bandeau[6] merveilleux
> Qui est le mien dans le colin-maillard des blessures

> (Arms connected only to the exceptional danger
>   of the body made for love
> Whose belly summons sighs detached from thickets
>   full of veils
> And who has nothing earthly but the immense frozen
>   truth of the sleighs of looks on the all-
>   white space
> Of that which I shall not see again
> Because of a marvelous band
> Which is mine in the blindman's buff of wounds, p. 88)

And once again by the interconnections of the Surrealist spirit, the distance experienced between the opposite poles of the image or the opposite moods of the poem which are joined in an insufferable/marvelous compound is a distance easily translated in terms of a voyage as the distance between Rimbaud's *Je* and his *autre* can be said, poetically, to inspire (or even to produce) not only the *Illuminations* but also the journey of the "Bateau ivre." At least four of the poems in the collection *Le Revolver à cheveux blancs* alone are centered on images of motion and journeys.

And the first "La Mort rose," actually begins as an echo of "Le Bateau ivre":

> Les pieuvres ailées guideront une dernière fois
> la barque
>
> (The winged devil-fish will guide the boat one
> last time)

before moving on to active descriptions (of the horizon opening, of a girl dancing, of the poet climbing, then walking at a rapid pace), and a final loneliness characteristic of the Surrealist alternation between hope and despair.

A far more interesting poem, more complex and more explicitly involved with the literary adventure, is "Dernière levée," of which the "subject" is a letter whose stamp is obliterated by the Zodiac and where Breton's name is almost indecipherable. The atmosphere of uncertainty and menace continues:

> Quand elle me parviendra le soleil sera froid
> Il y aura des épaves sur la place Blanche
> Parmi lesquelles se distinguera mon courage
>
> (When it reaches me the sun will be cold
> There will be shipwrecks on the Place Blanche
> Among which my courage will stand out)

He opens the letter immediately, *"d'un coup de rame"* (literally, with an oar stroke, the expression *d'un coup*—at once—leading to the singularly appropriate image of the oar), and then his own voyage in the ship formed of the words never yet heard—and therefore marvelous—will correspond to the one which the letter has made to reach him. People will gather at the dramatic sight (*"coup de rame"* including the sound *"drame"*), as if the action of language were suddenly to be made a spectacle:

> Mais je ne m'arrêterai pas
> Les mots jamais entendus prendront le large
> Ils seront de paille enflammée et luiront dans
> une cage d'amiante
> Suspendue à l'arbre à devinettes

> (But I shall not stop
> The unfamiliar words will set out to sea
> Made of burning straw they will shine in an
>   asbestos cage
> Hung from the riddle tree, p. 109)

But the voyage was only predicted, and before the end, the scene once again shifts to waiting, to dreams disappointed (*"voiliers éteints"* = extinguished sailboats) or at least reduced in size, like the tiny sailboat on the puddle at the end of "Le Bateau ivre":

> La lettre que j'attends sera de la couleur des
>   voiliers éteints. . . .
> Qu'elle est de petites dimensions cette lettre
>   que j'attends
> Pourvu qu'elle ne s'égare pas parmi les grains
>   de poison
>
> (The letter I wait for will have the color of
>   extinguished sailboats. . . .
> How small it is this letter I am waiting for
> As long as it does not stray among the
>   specks of poison, p. 110)

Just after a lyric description of the letter's importance—in the news it contains the poet expects to find all he has lost, animals and their sudden metamorphoses, the stones he used to feel a danger to his voyage (*"pour me dépister,"* to throw me off the track), and the lights *"qui bercent les choses irréelles"* (which lull unreal things)— the rapid descrescendo in size is as spectacular as the imagined voyage of flaming straw in all its splendid ambiguity (the riddle-tree). The tiny physical dimensions of the final menace match those of the letter, as the still potential drama of one corresponds to that of the other.

Often the violent activity or potential activity within the poem, like the exclamations frequent in Breton's writings (*"On secoue!,"* *"Allo!," "Allons!," "Oh!," "Ah!"*) seem to be as much a way of forcing the reader's attention as of enlarging the interior distance. In "Les Attitudes spectrales," the atmosphere of ghostly calm one might have expected from the title is broken by people walking,

underground passages, a tramway, a ship, a car moving at high
speed, a gallop, while in a poem already mentioned, "Sur la route
qui monte et qui descend" (in whose title there is already all the
motion of ascent and descent), the running flame never stops
from the beginning to the end of the poem.

Excepting these poems from *Le Revolver à cheveux blancs,* the
poem which deals most directly with all the phenomena of action
is *Fata Morgana,* where, however, the action is no longer exterior
as in the poems so far discussed, but purely imaginary or dreamed;
the bed replaces the carriages and ships of the preceding poems,
and in fact the voyage is in every way more "marvelous," to use
the Surrealist terminology:

> Le lit fonce sur ses rails de miel bleu. . . .
> Le lit brûle les signaux il ne fait qu'un de tous
>   les bocaux de poissons rouges
> Il lutte de vitesse avec les ciels changeants
> Rien de commun tu sais avec le petit chemin de fer. . . .
> Le lit brûle les signaux il ne fait qu'un
>   de tous les bocaux de poissons rouges. . . .[8]
> Enfin tout est repris par le mouvement de la mer
> Non le lit à folles aiguillées ne se borne pas
>   à dérouler la soie des lieux et des jours
>   incomparables
>
> (The bed rushes by on its rails of blue honey. . . .
> The bed crashes the signals unites all
>   the goldfish bowls. . . .
> It races with the changing skies
> Nothing at all in common you know with the little
>   railroad. . . .
> The bed crashes the signals unites all
>   the goldfish bowls. . . .
> Finally all is gathered up by the movement of the sea
> No the bed with insane threads does not
>   limit itself to unwinding the silk of
>   incomparable days and places, p. 184)

The wildness of the needle might refer to the uncontrolled reactions of the train's speedometer as well as to the thread of silk,
the latter might be another version of the *fil conducteur* linking
marvelous incidents, and finally, the red stop signals through which

the imaginary bed/train crashes might be identified with the inseparable series of goldfish bowls, in turn similar to the cages whose bars are on the inside so that one can escape from them. This poem, like many of the most significant poems of Surrealism, is a rebellion against the generally accepted limits of imagination and of life. The reduction of the distance between realms which is the goal of Surrealist theory and language:

> Et les distances peuvent continuer à fondre
> (And the distances can continue to melt, p. 193)

is, by a typical paradox, the means for the enlargement of experience:

> Je commence à voir autour de moi dans la grotte
> Le vent lucide m'apporte le parfum perdu de
>   l'existence
> Quitte enfin de ses limites
> (I begin to look around me in the grotto
> The lucid wind brings me the lost perfume of
>   existence
> Finally free of its limits, p. 182)

VI   "Rideau rideau"

Of all the voyages presented or implied in Breton's poems, the most dramatic are these interior, imaginary, *invisible* ones. Penetrating behind (or beyond) the backdrop of the poem itself, they are not even bound by the limits of the poet's words. They reject the frame of the poem entirely, as in the image already quoted:

> Alors des étendues jettent l'ancre se déploient
> au fond de mon oeil fermé
>
> (Then great expanses cast anchor range themselves in the
> depths of my closed eye, p. 131)

Nor is the poet's vision in any way directed toward the reader; it is rather a spectacle he offers to himself, on an interior stage. All the characteristics of Surrealist personality and expression contribute to the poem as spectacle *for the poet,* such as the

emphasis on the dream and on its peculiar qualities of multiplication and ambiguity provoked within the atmosphere of the
marvelous he creates.

Je rêve je te vois superposé indéfiniment à toi-même
(I dream I see you superposed indefinitely upon yourself, p. 129)

Avec moi des bustes de cire plus beaux les uns que les autres mais
    parmi eux méconnaissable s'est glissé un buste vivant
(Around me wax busts each more beautiful than the next but a
    living bust has slipped in unrecognizably among them, p. 200)

Fata Morgana, which is above all a poem of this "merveilleux,"
shows these particular deformations of the real in many of its
parts; it is essentially a theatrical poem:

> Têtes de femmes qui se succèdent sur tes
>   épaules quand tu dors
>
> (Heads of women succeeding each other
>   on your shoulders when you sleep, p. 189)

Of course, we cannot tell the "real" head from the others, as, in
another poem, Breton cannot distinguish between *"toutes ces
femmes fausses et vraies"* (all these women true and false). And
if we should happen to look beyond the surface of the poem, we
cannot tell even where the poet is supposed to be—the poem is
not for us, nor is the poet to be our guide there. He and the
person whom he addresses are able to recognize each other:

> C'est toi c'est moi à tâtons sous l'éternel
>   déguisement
>
> (It is you it is I groping under the eternal
>   disguise, p. 190),

but to us only the disguise is apparent. Breton seldom lets us
forget the décor of the poem, or the fact that we see it, as it were,
second hand: that is, we are obviously looking at his deformed
(or marvelous) conception of the scenery. The confusion is further

complicated in the setting of the alchemical theater, since within
the obscurity of the occult, even the poet is not completely sure
of the true: (*"et c'est vrai ou presque"* and it is true or almost):

> Il arrive que le regard errant sur les dormantes
>   eaux du fossé circulaire
> Surprenne en train de se jouer le progrès
>   hermétique
> Tout de feinte et dont on ne saurait assez
>   redouter
> La séduction infinie. . . .
> Tout ce qui vient à souhait est à double face
>   et fallacieux
> Le meilleur à nouveau s'équilibre de pire. . . .
> Ceci dit la représentation continue
> Eu égard ou non à l'actualité

> (It happens that the look as it wanders over the
>   sleeping waters of the circular ditch
> Surprises hermetic progress taking place
> In complete pretense and whose infinite seduction
> Cannot be feared enough. . . .
> All that has been wished for is double-faced
>   fallacious
> The best again is balanced by the worst. . . .
> This said the representation goes on
> Whether it takes account of actuality or not, pp. 192–93)

An early poem, "Allotropie," is a prefiguration of the later
theatrical poems; opening, like *Nadja,* with a question of identity,
it then presents the dramatic outline of an ambiguous shadow,
perhaps of Breton who is both guilty and victimized, both disguised
and apparent in the permanent contrasts of Surrealist spectacle:

> Qui es-tu
> Ombre de malfaiteur sur les grands murs
> Ombre de signalisateur qui va plus loin que le signal
> Je suis le principal coupable
> En même temps que le principal innocent. . . .
> Quel maquillage
> Nul me reconnaîtra

(Who are you
Shadow of evildoer on the great walls
Shadower of signaler which goes farther than the
   signal
I am the guiltiest
And at the same time the most innocent. . . .
What makeup
No one will recognize me).

Finally, two poems from *Le Revolver à cheveux blancs* show with
great clarity (although with strong emotional overtones) the split
between subject and object of vision, or between Breton spectator
and character in the drama. "Rideau rideau," a brief theatrical-
poetic autobiography, shows Breton's life *played out* on stages
while he hisses at it from a prompter's box which is also a prison,
sometimes screaming, sometimes attempting suicide, feeling himself
at once separated from the scene and involved enough to re-experi-
ence the mental crises within the scenes:

Mais c'étaient des pays dans lesquels je m'étais
   perdu
(But those were countries where I had lost myself, p. 99)

A man masked with the poet's features and free, as he himself is
not initially, wanders up and down; when suddenly the complete
liberty *of dream* is granted to the poet (so that he can chase away
all the *"apparences réelles,"* the *real* appearances which form his
paradoxical universe), the poem ends in an atmosphere of
catastrophe absent from the earlier poem. Silhouetted against the
white wall of the basement, surrounded by the aura of the *merveilleux,* appears the poet's other self, outlined in fire and with a
bullet piercing his heart. Once more, he is the criminal and the
victim, in his own theater.

The positive equivalent of both these poems, and the possible
key to their significance (as Breton would say) is the famous
"Vigilance," a dream poem where the poet sets fire to his own
dreaming body (that is, he *dreams* of setting fire to his own body
as he dreams, in an endless, or marvelous, circle) in a mood of
peace, quiet, and resolve; in this scene he is purified by the patient
beaks of the birds of fire and at last, leaving behind him all the

heavy, material, and human dross, enters the ideal ark of the universe. No longer guilty, or innocent, since he is not now judged by human standards, he is granted a paradisiacal vision of the center of things and finally possesses the connecting link he has sought so long: *"Je tiens le fil"* (I hold the thread). Here the poet identifies himself with the alchemist and with the matter on which the alchemist works, with the unpurified and then with the purified, as well as with the agent of the purification. Tzara's *Homme approximatif* undergoes a similar purification by fire and *transmutation* after his long voyage. In both cases, poet and poem, actor and spectacle unite beyond the framework of literature. More than any other, this is the experience of Surrealist poetry.

VII   "Une fois surtout une fois"

> C'en est fait du présent du passé de l'avenir
> Je chante la lumière unique de la coincidence
> (The present past future are finished
> I sing the unique light of coincidence, p. 139)

The hourglasses and clocks occasionally present in Breton's early poems play very little part in his later poems. The sails of the boat in "La Mort rose" are made of "his one day hour by hour," but the nature of the Surrealist vision with its perpetual balance prevents any emphasis on the *development* of time. As Breton remarks in his attack on novelistic descriptions, it is better not to speak at all about the *"moments nuls"* of one's life, the totally insignificant periods. The usual attitude of Surrealism is, then, that the spectacle is permanent and that one's action upon it is constant. It neither *changes,* nor develops, although it may alternate. The distinction is essential.

If there seems to be a progression from the transient, non-purified state of raw matter to the purified, eternal state gained by the process of transmutation, it is a progression which must be continually re-created. Just as Breton is forced to refuse the idea of a revolution toward a specific end which, being reached, might then invalidate the idea of further revolution, he must—in order to preserve the continual movement of the Surrealist gesture— insist on the cyclical nature of all Surrealist action:

Je coupe et je fends le bois de cet arbre qui
   sera toujours vert
. . .
L'avenir n'est jamais

(I chop and I split the wood of this tree which
   will always be green
. . .
The future is never, p. 81)

One never arrives at the future, and yet it controls many of the visions within the poems ("Rendez-vous," "La Mort rose," "Les Attitudes spectrales"), and occasionally, as in the poem just quoted, the situation presented would only be possible in that future which is never supposed to be.

Les rideaux qui n'ont jamais été levés
Flottent aux fenêtres des maisons qu'on construira

(The curtains which have never been raised
Flutter in the windows of the houses yet to be built, p. 81)

No prejudice from the past weighs down the present, nor does the present limit the future, which will never be sufficiently tangible to disprove prophecies or to interfere with dreams. All the tenses of Surrealism coincide in a complete liberty:

La vie comme un passeport vierge

(Life like a virgin passport)

By the stubborn denial of chronological separation, the full dualistic intensity of any particular moment can be felt, and can be felt as eternal:

A la vie à la mort cours à la fois les deux lièvres
Cours ta chance qui est une volée de cloches
   de fête et d'alarme

(For life for death chase both rabbits at
   the same time
Take your chance which is a pealing of bells of
   celebration and alarm, p. 162)

> A la vie à la mort ce qui commence me précède
> et m'achève

> (For life for death what begins precedes me
> and finishes me, p. 189)

The Surrealist attitude is as concrete as any other: a certain tree-lined square exists so that we can cross it at a certain angle *"dans la vraie vie"* (in real life), and in the forest seen right at this moment through the window, *if we had the key,* we would find the only clearing important for us. It is true that in an early poem of *Poisson soluble,* Breton expresses a certain *ennui* at the interchangeability of hours, persons, and events:

> Ce Monsieur, vous ne le connaissez pas? c'est
> M. Lemême. Je vous présente Madame Madame . . .
> Nous y sommes: l'ennui, les belles parallèles,
> ah! que les parallèles sont belles sous la
> perpendiculaire de Dieu

> (You don't know this man?
> it's Mr. Thesame. May I present Mrs. Mrs. . . .
> Here we are: tedium, the beautiful parallels,
> oh! how beautiful the parallels are under
> the perpendicular of God, p. 56)

And in "Le Verbe être" he laments the despair of four o'clock, of midnight, of the everlasting sameness of experience:

> C'est une corvée de jours de moins qui va
> encore faire ma vie

> (one day less upon another is going to
> make up my life again, p. 86)

Nevertheless, in the later poems, the combination of unique and interchangeable finds its resolution in the profoundly optimistic theory already touched on: "Toujours pour la première fois":

> Toi que je découvre et qui restes pour moi
> toujours à découvrir[9]
> (You whom I discover and who remain for me
> always to discover, p. 145)

All the moments are new within the unique love to which these lines refer, within the Surrealist paradise, where, since evil does not exist, the apple tree is no longer an agent of damnation: "Tout le pommier en fleur de la mer/All the apple tree flowering with sea."

According to Breton, the task of the Surrealist poet is to help us understand that *"le phénix/est fait d'éphémères"* (that the phoenix is made of ephemerids), that the marvelous phenomenon of rebirth does not necessarily imply the phenomenon of ennui—for the moments, which do not last, are fresh, unique, never the same, even if they are at the same time eternal. No more revealing study of the Surrealist spirit can be undertaken than the study of the endings of Breton's poems. Almost every one is what would be traditionally called a perfect ending, suited exactly to the mood of the poem or to its themes or images, and yet from each ending the entire poem, or another unique and yet similar, could begin afresh. Thus, for example, the poem which begins *"Toujours pour la première fois"* ends with the same line, and yet, according to the sense of the poem, it is no longer the same line.[10]

Fata Morgana, the poem which best illustrates the importance Breton accords to the interior voyage, to the unique moment of perception, to the constant *play* and the spectacle of the marvelous:

> C'est la pièce sans entr'acte le rideau levé
>   une fois pour toutes sur la cascade
> (It's the play with no intermission the
>   curtain raised once and for all on the cascade, p. 185)

is, just as clearly, the poem of Surrealist hope which goes far beyond a fairy tale.

> Ce matin la fille de la montagne tient sur ses
>   genoux un accordéon de chauves-souris blancs
> Un jour un nouveau jour . . .
> (This morning the mountain girl holds on her knees
>   an accordeon of white bats
> A day a new day . . ., p. 179)

The motif *"un nouveau jour"* is repeated, and every time it is new. Love does not lose in not changing its visage, Breton reiterates here, nor does life; they are always seen for the first time, no matter when. The luxurious spectacle *watched* by the people who remain *"dans les ombres du décor"* (in the shadows of the scenery) to contemplate a great feast contrasts vividly with the total simplicity and emotion of the poem's end, in which the poet is involved:

> . . . Plus ne m'est rien rien ne m'est plus
>   Oui sans toi
> Le soleil
> (. . . Nothing means anything to me to me nothing means
>   Yes without you
> The sun, p. 195)

The final image of the sun answers the initial image of the morning, the love denies the *spectacle,* and the poet-hero,

> Un homme grand engagé sur un chemin périlleux
> Cet homme parmi tant d'autres brusquement semblables
> (A tall man started on a perilous path
> This man among so many others suddenly
>   similar, p. 188),

does not this time force the reader outside of his own theater.

Finally, it is on the sense of the unique as eternal that the poetic structure of Breton's Surrealism is based. This is the key to all the fields and the resolution of all the dualities inherent in the Surrealist attitude. And it is at this point that the transmutation of spectator into participant could begin:

> Tu verras l'horizon s'entrouvrir . . .[11]
> (You will see the horizon start to open . . ., p. 71)

CHAPTER 10

"Le coup d'aile"

Mais où sont les neiges de demain? (But where are the snows of tomorrow?)

I *The Future of the Imagination:* "Il y aura une fois" (*1932*)
and "Situation surréaliste de l'objet" (*1935*)

Of all the links created or perceived by Surrealism (and, by a further link, those verbs are identified in Surrealist thought), the one joining imagination and life is unquestionably the most important. More than any other contemporary writer, Breton devotes his fullest attention to the elucidation and the celebration of that link. *"Il y aura une fois"* ("Once upon a time there will be"), the essay introducing his most widely read collection of poems, *Le Revolver à cheveux blancs,* states the Surrealist creed: that which is imagined may someday be. The only path to the marvelous and the only remedy for the dessication inflicted by the scientific mentality which insists on stressing the known to the detriment of the unknown, the human imagination must be valued at its proper worth. Not a gift, but a skill which must be *conquered,* the imagination

does not have to humble itself before life. . . . There will always be, especially among the ideas called accepted and ideas . . . whose acceptance we must bring about,[1] a difference capable of making the imagination mistress of the mental situation. . . .

The imaginary is what tends to become the real. (*Le Revolver,* p. 11)

At this point, Breton speaks of the problem of "the transformation of energy." Our failing to use the practicality of the imagination is as absurd as it would be for us to do without electricity in order to let water we had previously harnessed for electric power go back to being a waterfall.

It is all a matter of choice. The Surrealists would initiate us, whenever and wherever possible, to the poetic procedure (*"la démarche poétique"*), which will give imagination free scope. This procedure, as Breton describes it in his important essay of 1935, "Situation surréaliste de l'objet: situation de l'objet surréaliste," can be summed up in the following way: first, to rely less upon the exterior object as such and to consider nature "only in its relationship with the interior world of consciousness" (*Manifestes,* p. 312). Second, to examine all the results of the processes we would ordinarily consider arbitrary (for instance, the results of automatic practices, or of the "objective chance" which finds us doing certain things without our having planned it). We will, Breton assures us, find the results to be not in the slightest arbitrary, but rather, necessary. The connections between interior and exterior, between subjective and objective, in whichever direction they may seem to move, are *in reality* connections of the marvelous. Finally, the poetic imagination must remain free of the weight of logical habits of thought. The poet must, to this end, persevere in his effort to separate poetry from prose by means of the metaphor. Breton blames the very limited use of the metaphor ("this marvelous instrument") for the "poetic nullity" of the so-called classic centuries of poetry. Free also of any practical end seen in advance, of any concern for narration, the poet can work for the predominance of the pleasure principle over the reality principle, for the abolition of the *moi* in the *soi,* for the dialectical conciliation of the terms perception and representation. The sense in which the poetic imagination can be called upsetting (*"bouleversant"*) or revolutionary, is that, once having perceived, it calls imperiously for something in the outside world to answer its *prior* interior perception. And, Breton concludes, "It can be predicted that, to a great extent, this something *will be"* (*Manifestes,* p. 333). In its turn, moreover, this prediction just quoted is itself an answer to the title of the 1932 essay "Il y aura une fois," a phrase which recurs in a still more positive version eleven years later in the poem "Les Etats-Généraux" as part of an interior refrain: "IL Y AURA TOUJOURS . . .," which is set in a more imposing size of type than the rest of the poem. Touched neither by the

moments of ennui nor by the moments of personal despair, such
as the following:

> Je ne crois pas que le progrès s'opère dans la
>   direction du sens
> La confiance manque
>
> . . .
> J'ai comme un pressentiment de l'asile
> Des fuites sans mon éclat personnel
> Qui est un peu déchiqueté
>
> (I do not think that progress is made as to meaning
> Confidence is lacking
>
> . . .
> I have a foreboding of the asylum
>   Of escapes leaving behind the brilliance
>   of my personality
>   Which is a little tattered, "Le Volubilis et je sais
>   l'hypoténuse"),

Breton's certainty and his faith in his own predictions echo
throughout all his work.

II   *The Operation of Poetic Intuition:*

"Du Surréalisme en ses oeuvres vives" (*1955*)

Breton's essay on the state of Surrealism considers its accomplishments and its goals in the light of a perspective closer to that of
Arcane 17 than to that of the earlier essays. In fact, much of his
later work lays more stress upon the occultation of Surrealism
than upon the poetic work to be done, heard, and understood by
all, the latter optimism having been exemplified by the conclusion
of the *Vases communicants*.

The Surrealist movement had its origin in an operation on
language, Breton explains—language considered not only as the
expression of unconscious desire (an aspect unduly emphasized
because of the exaggerated interest in automatic writing) but, and
in this perspective, even more importantly, as the basic matter
(*"matière première"*) of creation. In the occult philosophy which
Surrealism admires and emulates:

enunciation is at the origin of everything, and therefore, "the name has to *germinate,* so to speak, otherwise it is false." The principal contribution of Surrealism, in poetry as in the plastic arts, is to have so exalted this germination as to make everything else appear ridiculous. (*Manifestes,* p. 358)

Here also Breton reiterates Surrealism's attitude toward elective love as a sufficient negation of the supposed dualism of the soul and the body. In spite of the difficulties caused by exterior forces of division, the promise held out by *"l'amour-passion"* is kept. In the world to which it opens the gates, there is neither sin nor evil. Third, the Surrealist image, the generator of sparks and the agent of transparency, is at the same time a proof of the actuality of what Breton calls elsewhere the sublime point, confirming that "all that is high is like what is low" and "all that is within is like what is without." The dualities are overcome and the world becomes less opaque by the poetic operation. And last, the *poetic intuition* as it is freed in Surrealism from all its constraints not only assimilates "all of the known forms but creates new forms" in the processes of generation and germination already described. Here Breton refers in turn to Schopenhauer, Gérard de Nerval, Charles Fourier, and René Guénon, in describing various aspects of this mystic intuition, which is able to "embrace all the structures of the world, manifest or not. It alone provides us with the thread which can lead back to the path of Gnosis, as knowledge of suprasensible Reality, 'invisibly visible in an eternal mystery' " (*Manifestes,* p. 363).

III   *Indication, Image, and Key*

> Il y a un message au lieu d'un lézard sous
>   chaque pierre
>
> (Instead of a lizard, there is a message under
>   each stone, *Poèmes,* p. 37)

Like Baudelaire, Breton sees the world as a "forest of signals." Like Rimbaud, he would make of poets seers or *"voyants."* Like the alchemists and mystics, he believes in analogical operations for transmuting the raw material of language. Like a long series of

French writers, he exhibits in his prose and in his poetry a complicated eloquence which keeps the reader at a distance while
totally involving him within the text.

But Breton's particular personality as a writer lies somewhere
else, and in view of the deliberate difficulties posed by Surrealism,
it is not hard to predict that this "place" or unique *position* will
be easy neither to describe nor to appreciate. Not the least
difficulty is the apparent simplicity of the concern. In *Les Etats-
Généraux,* for instance, Breton speaks of his fascination with the
image in the following highly "unpoetic" lines:

> Les images m'ont plu c'était l'art
> À tort décrié de brûler la chandelle par les
>   deux bouts
>
> (Images have appealed to me it was the art
> Mistakenly despised of burning the candle at
>   both ends, *Poèmes,* p. 219)

Not only does the concept seem simplistic, to say the least, but
the verse is extremely awkward, especially when it is contrasted
with the major part of Breton's poetry, at once moving and
intricate. Why should a man of such extraordinary intelligence
and subtlety take such an unintellectual delight in "images" as
childish as the one he sometimes chooses, or is *given* to see?

And yet, of course, the answer is already implied in the question. Because it is an anti-intellectual exercise. Because the freedom of the Surrealist imagination depends on just that loosing
of intellectual bonds, so that poetry can begin. But again (lest
one's intellectual memory bring in the *"abêtissez-vous"* Pascal recommended), it is not so simple. Within the revolution against the
intellectual there is an interior theater of complexities, as within
some of Breton's poems there is an interior structure to mock, or,
more rarely, to *underline* the exterior structure (see, for instance,
"Noeuds des miroirs," where a pseudo-botanical formula "combats
the noise of the gallop" or *Les Etats-Généraux,* where the inner
refrain is finally integrated with the outer). The "dramatic com-
plicities" he mentions are those relationships which germinate like
the alchemical language itself into a series of multiple meanings

forming, in an endless succession, the material for a future transformation of language: and this cycle is the stuff of poetry.

Breton's faith that the power generated by the work of poetry
is sufficient to act on the universe is perhaps a childish faith, as is
the absolute assurance that to every field or "locked wood" there
is a key, and that under every stone there is a message. But the
Surrealist belief, to which all are finally not called, depends on
this seeming childishness for its difficulty, and on its difficulty for
its unique, inimitable strength.

CHAPTER 11

Conclusion

Le jugement est un pont jeté mais il n'est pas
si beau que mon vertige

(Judgment is a bridge laid down, but it is not
as beautiful as my dizziness, "Camp volant")

Far more valuable than all the "projects for bridges" over the
frightening abyss, more valuable than all the well-meaning
approbation of the Surrealist endeavor and even than the healthier
hatred of that endeavor by those who do not share it, is the
spontaneous *vertige* suffered and enjoyed by the participants of
the Surrealist work. As their beauty is a convulsive one, dualistic
and not simple, so their pleasure is a double pleasure just as in the
poems of Breton the laceration doubles the luxury.

If there is one quality which sets Breton apart from his con-
temporaries and his predecessors, it is this intense energy which
comes through all his writing and seems to have pervaded his life
as well. His desperate optimism, his striking refusal of the ordinary
ways of thinking he found limited for the search of the *fil conducteur* to link all the limitless fields he has opened, his personality
(usually described as "magnetic"), all these are uncompromising,
dramatic, and, at their best, contagious. Breton, and Surrealism as
he conceived it and guided it, stand out as unique examples of *total*
involvement and complete passion, a fact which is probably responsible for the adverse judgments passed on Breton, on the Surrealists, and on Surrealism as a movement. Passion may look
ridiculous to the dispassionate, and complete involvement childish
to the uninvolved.

Breton would not have cared. The re-creation of the work, the
celebration of the festival are *inner spectacles* and are not touched
by outside judgments. *"L'amour fou"* is beautiful because it is

"*fou.*" Breton's ultimate and incalcuable significance, his over-whelming appeal for the passionate and the young, lie above all in his deliberate challenge, quoted near the beginning of this present study: Je tiens à passer pour un fanatique

(I insist on being considered extremist)

Notes and References

Preface

1. "Le temps" meaning both weather and time: Breton and the other Surrealists use all the ambiguities possible.
2. In deference to the subject of this book, Dada will be discussed in the past tense and Surrealism, in the present.
3. Except *within* the limits of the forms.

Chronology

1. Although it is possible, as Bruce Morrissette suggests in his study, *The Great Rimbaud Forgery: the Affair of "La Chasse Spirituelle"* (Saint Louis, Washington University Studies, 1956) that Breton had also a reason "exterior" to the text for suspecting it to be false.

Chapter One

1. The spelling is an obvious mockery of such a profession.
2. Claude Mauriac, *André Breton,* Ed. de Flore, 1949, p. 345.
3. Victor Crastre, *André Breton, Arcanes,* 1952, p. 194.

Chapter Two

1. The numbers between the parentheses refer to pages within the book under discussion, in the edition quoted in the bibliography.
2. Breton also quotes Lautréamont's attack against Pascal: "The fly does not reason very well at the present time. A man is buzzing in his ears." (Pascal, in order to show the variability and weakness of the human mind, had said the reverse of this. The Surrealists stand with man, against anything which would seem to depreciate his value, or the strength of his imagination.)
3. Neither are any of the collaborative works: *Les Champs magnétiques* or the plays *Vous m'oublierez, S'il vous plaît* (with Philippe Soupault), *L'Immaculée conception* or *Notes sur la Poésie* (with Paul

Eluard), *Ralentir travaux* (with René Char and Paul Eluard), *Martinique charmeuse de serpents* (with André Masson), etc. In accordance with Surrealist principles of choice, anything which did not seem of particular importance at this moment and from this point of view was simply omitted.

4. The similarities and differences between Dada and Surrealism are not treated here in any detail, although they are as important as they are interesting. For a brief discussion of them, see Michel Sanouillet, *Dada à Paris* (Pauvert, 1965), Herbert Gershman, *The Surrealist Revolution in France* (Ann Arbor, Michigan, 1968), or my *Poetry of Dada and Surrealism: Aragon, Breton, Tzara, Eluard, Desnos* (Princeton, Princeton University Press, 1970).

Chapter Three

1. It is this crusade which Jules Monnerot describes as the "impossible possible." See *La Poésie moderne et le sacré,* Gallimard, 1945.

Chapter Four

1. Arthur Rimbaud, Symbolist poet, was haunted by the split between the I who speaks and the I who listens as "I speak": *Je est un autre*—I (who is) another, that is, I am, to myself, *the other.*

2. Which are "sadistic," in the strongest meaning of the term, but are followed, in the second part of the work by *Poésies,* the exact opposite of the *Chants:* alternation (as in the Surrealist lanaguage of opposites), recantation, forgery, joke? The mystery is unsolved.

3. Because it includes the contraries, on which the whole attitude and style of both movements are based, because it is essentially mobile, and for a number of other reasons. The notion is discussed at length in most of the books on the movements. Of course, during the more politically committed periods of Surrealism, the references to dialectic take on a slightly different connotation.

4. See the *Lettres de guerre de Jacques Vaché* (K, 1949), with four prefaces by Breton (1919, 1924, 1940, 1948). Vaché, an extraordinary personage, at least as Breton describes him, is the inventor of *umour.* As an example of it, he gives the following statement: "IT IS IN THE ESSENCE OF SYMBOLS TO BE SYMBOLIC," and the following definition:

I think it is a sensation—I was about to say a SENSE—that too—of the theatrical uselessness (and joylessness) of everything. WHEN ONE KNOWS.
And so that is why enthusiasms—(first of all, they are noisy)—*of others* are hateful. . . ."

And, in another place: "GOD IS ABSURD—for everything is contradictory, right? . . ."

In *his Dada à Paris,* Michel Sanouillet minimizes the great attraction Vaché is supposed to have had for Breton as a myth on Breton's part, invented in order to discount the importance of Tristan Tzara. In any case, the letters of Vaché are illuminating for certain sides of Breton's early character.

5. *"enlaçant,"* in the sense of "drawing one in."

6. "Nous embrassons tout, mais nous n'étreignons que du vent."

7. As an example, at the March 1968 exhibition held at the Museum of Modern Art on "Dada, Surrealism, and Their Heritage," there were protests in several newspapers and demonstrations on the spot against the "MUSEUM/MAUSOLEUM." Parallel accusations were made against the speakers at a "symposium" held in conjunction with the exhibition, on the grounds that to discuss Surrealism within such a setting is to dig its grave, make its autopsy, and so on.

8. Because its "lesson" was that the French nation should have more children, both the appeal to nationalism and to motherhood judged abhorrent from the Dada/Surrealist point of view.

9. A later essay, published in the Surrealist journal *Minotaure,* states the case for "Le Merveilleux contre le mystère," Surrealism favoring the former. Gradually, Breton seems to move more to the side of the mystics; see the comments on *Arcane 17* and the essay "Du Surréalisme en ses oeuvres vives."

10. Here I am indebted to a discussion with Madame Marie-Claire Dumas, who is preparing a work on Desnos.

11. See the present proliferation of works on concrete poetry: *An Anthology of Concrete Poetry,* ed. Emmett Williams, Pierre Garnier's *Spatialisme et poésie concrète,* etc.

Chapter Five

1. See the first chapter for a very rapid discussion of the problem of Surrealist alternations: between the will to share the Surrealist experience and the contrary, and sometimes simultaneous, desire not to distribute the *pain maudit aux oiseaux.*

2. Not in all cases; see the remarks on Lautréamont and Rimbaud in "Pour Dada," *Les Pas perdus* (mentioned in Chapter 1).

Chapter Six

1. For a discussion of the importance of electrical imagery in Breton's writings, see Julien Gracq, *André Breton, quelques aspects de l'écrivain,* Corti, 1948. In his "Chasse spirituelle," Breton states cate-

gorically: "What matters to us is what determines the fusion of the mind and the heart into a verbal or plastic mold which shows itself from some perspective electrically appropriate to it" (*La Clé*, p. 140).

2. Breton quotes here an article of Lo Duca, "L'Art et le fou."

3. Passive, in the sense that the medium is passive, in order to remain open to the message of the marvelous.

4. In a footnote to this passage, Breton tells how the writer Raymond Roussel (a writer admired by the Surrealists) went much further in this way of thinking; having embarked for the South Seas, he then refused to get off the ship when it arrived at Tahiti. (One more example of the unknown preferred to the known.)

5. Who is for this reason and others closely associated with Surrealism. For a more detailed account, see my *Surrealism and the Literary Imagination: Gaston Bachelard and André Breton* (The Hague, Mouton, 1966).

6. See the discussion about the volume of Resistance poetry called *L'Honneur des poètes* and the essay repudiating it, *Le Déshonneur des poètes* by Benjamin Péret. The conception of honor is plainly different.

7. From René Guénon, *Aperçus sur l'initiation*, quoted in Breton's essay "La Nuit du Rose Hôtel."

Chapter Seven

1. Compare the equally definite style of: "La beauté sera CON-VULSIVE ou ne sera pas."

Chapter Eight

1. Breton mentions here Lautréamont's personal disappearance behind his work, but for him such a feat seems *supernatural* (always to be contrasted with *surréel*); he himself would not respect anyone who tried now to undertake the same thing.

2. In another passage of *Nadja* (p. 49), Breton explains his affection for the Marché aux Puces as a place for finding, as one cannot in other places, certain objects which are "out of style, in pieces, useless, almost incomprehensible, in short perverse in the sense I mean it and as I love the term. . . ." These objects, like the "signal facts," can be put in no logical order and are a mockery of any order we might wish to bestow on them.

3. Breton, in fact, accuses himself for having "betrayed" his own personal attraction to the actress Blanche Derval. Not to profit from all the "marvelous" sensations is to fall short of the Surrealist ideal.

4. There is no good translation for the French *"faire la part du feu"*

(at least, I have not found one here). It is a counsel of moderation: give something its due, cut your losses, etc. Compare the following passage from *Les Vases communicants* (p. 144): "To the extent that I got out of the way of cars, that I did not permit myself to try out a firearm to see how it worked . . . I paid this world the greatest compliment."

5. Literally, a *fil conducteur,* a conducting wire; Breton is faithful to the imagery of electricity. The same image is applied to the distant elements of an image, and to any bringing together, an action to which Surrealism can be considered to have devoted itself in large part.

6. That the analysis should be carried on between two people fits, of course, the traditional psychological pattern and is also highly appropriate to Surrealism, which is more of a group phenomenon than an isolated one.

7. Breton gives an interesting interpretation of the dream within a dream as (roughly speaking) a process of making more *unreal* that on which the dreamer would not want to confer the greater reality of the first-level dream.

8. Here Breton disavows his own greatness in any field at all.

9. This underlining is mine; the other two are in the text.

10. From an article on Jacques Herold, in *Cahiers d'art,* Oct. 1947; the comparison made at this point between the crystal and the coral (or the crystal in the sea) is doubly interesting in view of all Breton's other references to the power of water—to the soluble fish, for instance, and to the water he imagines paralyzing the newest machines, imposing its own conditions from a position of greater strength.

11. There is often this total and obvious opposition, a point discussed in the last chapter here. Compare with other images, such as the one already mentioned in Noah's Ark to which Breton would have the crow return instead of the dove, or that of the black sand he chooses as the ideal setting for his dreams, instead of the white sand he used to prefer, etc.

12. And Breton emphasizes the importance of the loss of an actual child (physical or psychological) in both Elisa's case and in his own.

Chapter Nine

1. "Cours-les-Toutes." The contrast of the machine and rust, or the effect of rust, links this image to Breton's wish that water could paralyze all the newest machines.

2. Identification, and not likened to—*is* and not *is like*—because in Surrealism, the *"comme"* is often suppressed, to make the shock more powerful.

3. The visual balance is paralleled by the exact repetition of words.

4. A pun on earthworms: *"Ver de terre."*

5. Tristan Tzara, *Sept Manifestes Dada,* Pauvert, 1963, p. 107.

6. *"Bandeau"* refers to the blindfold in blindman's buff and at the same time to a diadem (allied to the notion of the marvelous).

7. Several of Breton's early poems have the rhythm and the vocabulary of Rimbaud; the voyage on the inside of the poet's eye is similar in feeling to the image of the young boy in Rimbaud's "Les Poètes de sept ans," who is *"écrasant son oeil darne."* Compare with this poem the following:

> Sous le bandeau de fusées
> Il n'est que de fermer les yeux
> Pour retrouver la table du permanent (p. 93)

8. Compare Eluard's *"ta langue dans le bocal de ta voix."*

9. Not "rediscover," since it is always for the first time.

10. For another circular poem, see "La Forêt dans la hache."

11. Literally "open halfway," like the *"porte entr'ouverte"* in *Les Vases communicants:* it implies the marvelous and the communication with it as the simpler *"ouvrir"* would not.

Chapter Ten

1. "Faire recevoir," an expression like Eluard's *"voir et faire voir,"* *"donner à voir,"* etc. The image implies the seer sharing his vision, making of others seers also.

Selected Bibliography

SOME PRIMARY SOURCES

(The place of publication is Paris unless otherwise noted.)

1919 *Mont de Piété,* Au Sans Pareil
1920 *Les Champs magnétiques* (with Philippe Soupault) (reprinted with the plays *Vous m'oublierez* and *S'il vous plaît,* also written in collaboration), NRF, 1968
1923 *Clair de terre,* Coll. Littérature
1924 *Les Pas perdus,* NRF (reprinted in 1945)
Manifeste du surréalisme, suivi de *Poisson soluble,* Editions Kra
1928 *Le Surréalisme et la peinture,* NRF (reprinted, with additions and revisions, 1965)
Nadja, NRF (reprinted with revisions, 1963)
1930 *Ralentir travaux* (in collaboration with René Char and Paul Eluard (Editions Surréalistes)
Second manifeste du Surréalisme, Editions Kra
L'Immaculée Conception (in collaboration with Paul Eluard), Editions Surréalistes; reprinted, Pierre Seghers, 1961
1931 *L'Union libre* (no author, place given)
1932 *Misère de la poésie—"L'affaire Aragon" devant l'opinion publique,* Editions Surréalistes
Le Revolver à cheveux blancs, Editions des Cahiers Libres
Les Vases communicants, Editions des Cahiers Libres (reprinted, NRF, 1955, 1967)
1934 *Qu'est-ce que le surréalisme?* Bruxelles, René Henriquez
L'Air de l'eau, Editions Cahiers d'Art
Point du jour (texts from 1924 to 1933) NRF
1936 *Notes sur la Poésie,* (in collaboration with Paul Eluard) G.L.M.
1937 *L'Amour fou,* N.R.F. (reprinted 1945)
1938 *Dictionnaire abrége du surréalisme* (in collaboration with Paul Eluard), Editions Beaux-Arts
Trajectoire du rêve, Cahiers GLM, no. 7 (texts concerning the dream, compiled by Breton)
Manifesto *Pour un Art Révolutionnaire Indépendant* (written in

collaboration with Leon Trotsky, signed by Breton and Diego Rivera)

1940 *Anthologie de l'humour noir,* Editions du Sagittaire. Last edition, Pauvert, 1966.

1941 *Fata Morgana,* Editions du Sagittaire

1944 *Arcane 17,* New York, Brentano's (reprinted, followed by *Enté d'Ajours,* Editions du Sagittaire, 1947)

1946 *Young Cherry Trees Secured Against Hares/Jeunes Cerisiers garantis contre les lièvres,* bilingual editions of poems, New York, View Editions (reprinted in Ann Arbor Paperbacks, Michigan, 1969)

1947 *Ode à Charles Fourier,* Editions de la Revue Fontaine
Yves Tanguy, New York, Editions Pierre Matisse

1948 *Martinique, charmeuse de serpents,* Editions du Sagittaire
Poèmes, NRF (anthology, 1919-48)

1950 *Almanach surréaliste du demi-siècle* (special number of *La Nef,* numbers 63/64)

1952 *Entretiens 1913–52* (with Andre Parinaud and others), NRF

1953 *La Clé des champs* (texts from 1937 to 1952), Sagittaire (reprinted, Pauvert, 1967)

1954 *Farouche à quartre feuilles* (in collaboration with Lise Deharme, Julien Gracq and Jean Tardieu), Grasset

1957 *L'Art magique* (with Gérard Legrand), Club Français du Livre

1962 *Manifestes du surréalisme* (including first and second manifestoes, *Poisson soluble, Lettre aux voyantes, Position politique du surréalisme, Prolégomènes à un troisième manifeste du surréalisme ou non, Du surréalisme en ses oeuvres vives*), Pauvert

SELECTED SECONDARY SOURCES

(*On Breton and Surrealism*)

ALQUIÉ, FERDINAND. *Philosophie du surréalisme.* Flammarion, 1955. Thorough, analytic, particularly interesting for the reader who has already some acquaintance with the topic. "Before any critical development, before any reflection on itself, Surrealism proposes to us the hope of existence, and projects this existence in a sort of other world beyond natural life, another world however immanent in it, and seeming to reveal itself to the man who desires to seize the world under the aspect of the marvelous" (p. 15).

AUDOUIN, PHILIPPE. André Breton. Gallimand, 1970. Brilliant. Easily the best study, and the most faithful to Breton and to Surrealism.

BALAKIAN, ANNA. *Surrealism, the Road to the Absolute.* New York: Noonday Press, 1959, Random House, 1967. Brief discussion of the predecessors of Surrealism (Baudelaire, Lautréamont, Apollinaire, Reverdy), of the influences upon it (Freud, Hegel), of the Surrealist image and the Surrealist attitude. Surrealism seen as an "earthbound *mystique*."

———. *André Breton.* Oxford University Press (not seen).

BÉDOUIN, JEAN-LOUIS. *André Breton,* Poètes d'aujourd'hui, Seghers, 1950. Selection of texts with laudatory preface on Breton as a "disturbing meteor. . . ."

———. *Vingt ans de surréalisme, 1939–1959.* Denoël, 1961. Particularly for the more recent period; written by a Surrealist, from the Surrealist point of view.

BROWDER, CLIFFORD. *André Breton, Arbiter of Surrealism.* Geneva: Droz, 1968. "Life and works" study: a bit dry.

CARROUGES MICHEL. *André Breton et les donneés fondamentales du surréalisme.* Gallimard, 1950. Breton thought this was an excellent study. Lofty and eloquent-sentimental style like that of Breton himself. Discussion (by a Roman Catholic) of Breton's "dialectical humanism," of his image of the crystal, etc.: "that this far-off diamond should grow until it includes the entire universe and how could this be possible if this universe did not burn away all its impurities, if it did not break through all its limits to become a pure sphere of solar crystal?" (p. 87).

CAWS, MARY ANN. *Surrealism and the Literary Imagination: A study of Gaston Bachelard and André Breton.* The Hague: Mouton, 1966.

———. *The Poetry of Dada and Surrealism: Aragon, Breton, Tzara, Eluard, Desnos.* Princeton: Princeton University Press, 1970.

CIRLOT, JUAN EDUARDO. *Introducción al surrealismo.* Madrid: Revista del Occidente, 1953. "As we have indicated, Surrealism diverges from the dialectical idealism of Hegel inasmuch as it calls for the concrete possession of the world, in its totality and in each one of its parts, spheres, and possibilities" (p. 376).

CRASTRE, VICTOR. *André Breton,* Arcanes, 1952. Political point of view: that Breton finally gave up trying to appeal to youth, and that Surrealism came to see that "poetry cannot be made by all in the world we are given" (p. 81). This was its greatest failure. But on the whole, complimentary for Breton.

DUPLESSIS, YVES. *Le Surréalisme (Que sais-je).* P.U.F., 1950. Arranged by themes; a beginning for the "new" reader.

EIGELDINGER, MARC. *André Breton, essais et témoignages.* Neuchâtel: Baconnière, 1950. A few important essays of Breton, then comments by Gracq, Carrouges, Paulhan, etc.

FOWLIE, WALLACE. *Age of Surrealism.* Bloomington: Indiana University Press, 1960. A panorama—Lautréamont, Rimbaud, Mallarmé,

Apollinaire, Cocteau, Picasso—as well as Breton and Eluard. Some would object to the inclusion of Mallarmé and particularly of Cocteau in a book with Breton.

GERSHMAN, HERBERT. *The Surrealist Revolution in France.* Ann Arbor: University of Michigan Press, 1968 (and *Bibliography of the Surrealist Revolution in France*). Careful and reliable history, with brief sections on the Surrealist esthetic, art and Surrealism, etc., accompanied by illustrations, appendixes, and detailed notes. Nicely breezy style; personal, rather critical approach. Breton comes off not too well, except as a "publicist."

GRACQ, JULIEN [Louis Poirier]. *André Breton: quelques aspects de l'écrivain.* Corti, 1948. Concise, intelligent, interesting.

MASSOT, PIERRE DE. *André Breton le septembriseur.* Corti, 1967. Supersentimental.

MATTHEWS, J. H. *An Introduction to Surrealism.* University Park: Pennsylvania State University Press, 1965. Wide-ranging study of themes and techniques in Surrealist art, with frequent and interesting quotations from a variety of spokesmen. Surrealism as an attitude and as a "human mission."

————. *André Breton.* New York: Columbia University Press, 1967. Brief, clear.

MAURIAC, CLAUDE. *André Breton, essai.* Editions de Flore, 1949. Thin.

MONNEROT, JULES. *La Poésie moderne et le sacré.* Gallimard, 1945. Difficult, abstract. Recommended for "advanced" readers. "This poetry *opens out on* insanity, but also on the lyric-dialectic, the elaboration of a problematics of existence, impossible possibility, possible impossibility. It opens out on the tragic as on a sort of method which our being would use in order to be" (p. 176).

NADEAU, MAURICE. *Histoire du surréalisme,* Seuil, 1954. Volume II contains documents of Surrealism. (Translated in English, introduction by Roger Shattuck, Collier, 1967.) This book provokes, because of its title and historical attitude, the wrath of the present Surrealists.

Yale French Studies. Spring, 1964. Surrealism issue.

L'Esprit créateur. Spring, 1966. Surrealism issue.

NRF. *André Breton et le mouvement surréaliste.* Special number, April, 1967. See particularly the essays of Andre Pieyre de Mandiargues (on the Surrealist language), of Octavio Paz (on revelation, meditation, election), of Charles Duits (on the figure of Breton in 1943), of Michel Beaujour (on *Nadja*), and of Philippe Jaccottet (on the *oratory* nature of Breton's poems).

Index

(In entries of multiple items, the first item listed is considered the most important in the text. The meaning of the items given in French is apparent from the context.)

alchemy, 20, 28, 39, 55, 86, 98, 107, 115, 116
Alice, 59
alienation, 78
analogies, 54 (*see also* linking)
Apollinaire, 29, 36, 53, 78
Aragon, 18, 19
Arnim, 17, 43
Arp, 58
Artaud, 18, 22
automatic processes, 17, 24, 37, 44, 45, 50, 53, 64, 65, 72, 91, 114
autre chose, 52

Bachelard, 51
Baudelaire, 42, 80, 115

Caillois, 51
call, the, 44
Cézanne, 36
Char, 46
(de) Chirico, 45
communicating vessels, 8, 27, 59, 67, 68, 72, 78, 79, 114; door ajar, 63, 73
Communist party, 14, 15, 19, 79
condition, situation, 9, 16, 30, 32, 55, 60, 75, 113
connecting wire, linking, 8, 53, 61, 73, 88, 90, 102, 107, 112, 113, 118
content, latent, 8
continuity, 83, 84, 92 (*see also* communicating vessels; linking)
convulsive, *convulsionnaire,* 72, 98, 124
Crastre, 16

Crevel, 38
crystal, 8, 24, 41, 44, 45, 46, 47, 81; glass house, 63; transparency, 89, 115, 125

Dada, 14, 20, 28, 30, 31, 32, 33, 34, 35, 52, 81, 122
Dali, 45
dédoublement, 43
Derain, 62
Desnos, 18, 22, 35, 38, 39, 40
dialectic, 32, 46, 47, 59, 76, 113, 122
differentiation, separation, 63, 95; split, 8, 67, 105, 122, distance, 78, 101
difficulty, 50, 115
désorientation, *détournement, dépaysement,* 17, 43, 48, 52, 54, 57, 60, 60

Dostoevsky, 24
doubt, 34, 50, 82, 84
dualities, ambiguities, paradox, equivocal, contraries, complementarity, 18, 31, 32, 34, 40, 41, 44, 51, 52, 58, 66, 72, 77, 78, 82, 86, 92, 95-101, 104, 105, 108, 111, 115, 121, 122

electricity, short circuits, 51, 52, 112, 125
Eluard, 18, 39, 74, 95, 126
encounters, 9
Engels, 17, 75
enigma, 71, 72, 74
ennui, ennuyeux, 25, 64, 67, 109, 110, 114

equilibrium, 30, 43

Ernst, 22, 39, 43, 44

esthetics, estheticism, 13, 36, 37, 44, 67, 76, 79

Etiemble, 51

extreme, 23, 26, 119

faith, 25, 77, 80, 82, 84, 114, 117

famine, 20, 60

Ferry, 49   s

flag, 90

(La) Fontaine, 46

Fourier, 15, 90, 115

freedom, liberation, 9, 20, 30, 46, 55, 112

Freud, 11, 74

generosity, 16, 55 (see also openness)

Gnosis, 115

God, religion, Christianity, 29, 50, 52, 63, 74, 90, 123 (*see also* flag)

Gothic novel, 23, 51, 98

Guénon, 115, 124

Hamlet, 58

Hare, 15

hasard objectif, objet trouvé, coincidence, 53, 75 (*see also* encounter)

Hegel, 17, 46, 53, 81

Heraclitus, 17, 53

hostility, 46, 83

illumination, lucidity, 45, 50, 51, 59, 84, 86

immobility, paralysis, 24, 41, 49, 90, 125

inquiétude, trouble moderne, 30, 35, 57, 62; disturbance, 66; anguish, 53, 59, 86

insolite, 24, 82

interior model, 18, 58

inversion, 98

juxtaposition, 87

key, key to the fields, 29, 52, 82, 109, 111, 117

Keyserling, 44

knowledge, 36, 48

labyrinth, 46, 60

Lacan, 51

Lautréamont, 13, 17, 18, 31, 34, 57, 121, 123, 124

lêse-réalité, 58

lyric attitude, poetic attitude, 21, 60, 79, 90

madness, *fou, garde-fou,* 27, 28, 50, 62, 81, 82, 83, 118, 119

Magritte, 49

Mallarmé, 13, 57

Marx, 14, 18, 20, 72, 77

May, 1968, 15, 19

Meister Eckhardt, 17, 53

Mélusine, 86

mirror, 28, 54, 70, 97

Montaigne, 32

moral commitment, heroic concern, 22, 31, 55, 59, 60

Morise, 39

movement, fluctuation, 54, 66, 80, 96, 99, 102; fleeting, 90 (*see also* openness)

multiplicity, multiplication, 42, 80, 81, 116

museum, 35, 123

necessity, 33, 113; interior necessity, 8

Nerval, 115

occult, 26, 114

openness, 8, 9, 27, 28, 50, 51, 80; open realism, open rationalism, 51

Orient, the, 44

Pascal, 116, 121

passion, 56, 57, 115, 119

(la) pensée parlée, 25

Péret, 21, 124

Picabia, 35

Picasso, 45, 46, 159

(le) pli, 26, 39

plurality, proliferation, ramifications, expansion, 77, 92, 97, 104

point sublime, point faillible, 27, 28, 80, 82, 83, 84
positive, optimism, 20, 70, 109
possibility, 8
present, moment, 8, 9, 13, 46, 53, 71, 110, 121, 122
primitivism, 60, 75
Proust, 52
psychology, 73, 125

Racine, 31
receptivity, *disponibilité,* 25, 33; expectation, 57, 58, 78
récit de reves, 38
reduction, 23, 24, 74, 103
Renoir, 36
repetitions, 24, 88
Reverdy, 25, 87
revolt, revolution, 13, 19, 22, 23, 30, 32, 46, 48, 49, 50, 55, 56, 73, 76, 77, 79, 107, 113
Rimbaud, 17, 28, 31, 34, 39, 43, 57, 66, 99, 101, 115, 122, 123, 126
risk, danger, 34, 60, 65, 71
Romanticism, 27
Roussel, 124

Saint-Pol Roux, 42
Schopenhauer, 115
(se) tenir bien, 70
severity, stubbornness, uncompromising, nonacceptance, 18, 22, 26, 28, 49

signals, 63, 64; *faits-glissades, faits-précipices,* 65, 67
simplicity, 42, 44, 55, 57, 64, 92, 111
Soupault, 37, 121
spontaneous, 24, 48, 50, 66, 69

taste, bad, 23
tension, 87, 88
Theseus, 46
tornado, 67
translate, 42
transmutation, 107, 111
Trotsky, 19
Tzara, 14, 15, 18, 20, 30, 34, 35, 95, 97, 99, 107

unity, resolution, 44, 76, 108, 111
unknown, 23, 45
use, 19, 37

Vaché, 13, 14, 32, 122, 123
Valéry, 13, 52
valeur secouante, 18
vertige, 31, 43, 81, 118
Waldberg, 13
word, language, 28, 34, 39, 40, 41, 53, 91, 114, 115

youth, 15, 56, 61, 119

Appendix

Reading a Surrealist poem

Texts: "L' aigle sexuel exulte," "Il allait être cinq heures," "Ils vont tes membres" from *L' Air de l'Eau.*
Love and poetry as resolution of polarities, as regeneration and reproduction

A double rhythm of love as joining and suffering—theme
B markings of polarities and resolution
C luminosity, clarity

D suffering, danger
E color green (reproduction)
F sound: ambiguity, poetry

guiding images:

poem 1
l'aigle sexuel
  A

son aile descendante
son aile ascendante
  AB

joie dans l' exhalaison
de cette douleur AB

je prends l'empreinte de
la mort et de la vie
  BE

poem 2
un poignard dont le
manche de corail
bifurquera à l'infini
pour que ton sang et le mien
n'en fassent qu'un ABF

ce froissement de
fleurs et
d'aiguilles de glace
  B

poem 3
lit prismatique
  AC

un cri de l'hôpital
de la Maternité
  ADEF

des clochers
se rejoignent
  BF

jours clairs, miroir,
journal de verre
lumière électrique,
ce rayon, l'air
liquide C

manches de menthe
EF

incision de l'émeraude
donna naissance
au feuillage DE

étoile filante
C

un ver luisant
CF

faire éclater
les vitres CD (contrary of: hermétique)

comme une feuille
E

sourcils verts
EF

le chant des
vitriers CF

draps verts AEF

saule E

feuille glissante
et sans bords DE